T0137503

Let Us Pray...

PATRICIA A. COHEN

WESTBOW
PRESS*
A DIVISION OF THOMAS NELSON
& ZONDERVAN

WestBow Press books may be ordered through booksellers or by contacting:

WestBow Press
A Division of Thomas Nelson & Zondervan
1663 Liberty Drive
Bloomington, IN 47403
www.westbowpress.com
1 (866) 928-1240

Scripture taken from the King James Version of the Bible.

ISBN: 978-1-9736-7920-2 (sc)
ISBN: 978-1-9736-7919-6 (e)

Library of Congress Control Number: 2019917810

Print information available on the last page.

WestBow Press rev. date: 11/21/2019

Dedication

To my dad, Purnell Cohen who prayed every morning, on his knees for at least an hour before he exited his bedroom. He called people by their names and interceded before the Lord on their behalf. My dad went home to be with the Creator on Tuesday, July 23, 2019. Thank you, dad, and to God be the glory.

Foreword

The power of prayer makes the unseen, seen! The power of prayer makes the seen, obsolete! The power of an effectual fervent prayerful life changes the atmosphere wherever this life lives! For almost 25 years Evangelist Cohen was the sole caretaker of her father after a terrible automobile accident left him quadriplegic. Through prayer, she persevered seeing God restore her father back to walking on his own with the use of only a cane. Furthermore, during this time she prevailed and overcame cancer twice within less than two years while still caring for her dad. Knowing what God can and will do, she truly knows the power of prayer even through difficult, demanding and testing times. With this in mind, to pray for others comes naturally by the leading of the Lord.

The power of these prayers will lead and take you comparatively further in learning to trust in God. I can attest that if you embrace these prayers, your life will never the same. I believe that these life changing prayers will work for you by believing and trusting Jesus Christ.

Bishop Deloris McNeal Young, D.D.

Founder and Senior Pastor of the Greater Pentecostal Temple, Inc., in Hardeeville, South Carolina. She is the Lay Director for the Southeastern District and a Bishop of the Pentecostal Assemblies of the World (PAW), where she holds the distinct honor of being the first woman appointed to these positions in the state of Georgia, United States of America.

Acknowledgements

I am so appreciative to the leading ladies who helped guide my life: My mom, Mrs. Mae Bell Cohen, "Z"L"; Reverend Mother Derris Cargile, "Z"L", and Bishop Deloris M. Young, my Pastor and watchman for my soul. Also, Mrs. Mary Elizabeth Green-Cohen Winston and Mother Shirley Scott who informed me they typed out and catalogued each prayer received via text.

Preface

While in a minister's meeting one Saturday, I heard the various comments about the struggles different persons were going through. My heart went out to each of them, but I didn't quite know what I could do for them, except pray. We were in the season of Lent, a season of penitence, self-sacrifice, and soul searching. After thinking about it a few days, I was led by the Lord to daily send out a prayer to the ministers via text during this season. The next year I opened the prayers up to all the leaders of the church. As word got around in and out of the church, I was sending a prayer each day to a few hundred people, most I knew, many I did not (names were submitted by their loved ones).

My hope was that it would encourage the recipients to increase their own prayer life, that they would increase their prayers for others, and know that through faith in what they were praying and living works, their relationship with the Lord would grow.

Contents

Chapter One

Lent Prayers 2014

Monday, March 10

Let us pray, Lord, Thank You for opening our eyes to Your generous graces. Help us to treat ourselves like the wonder of Your creation we are. Amen.

Tuesday, March 11

Father, Thank you for all your many blessings that you bring us each day. Please help us be an example of Christ in our daily life and spread the good news to glorify you in Heaven. Amen.

Be grateful...faithful over a little, He'll make you ruler over much.

Wednesday, March 12

Thank You, Father, for helping me to be still in Your presence while praying and thanking You for hearing my cry. I am patiently waiting for You to move on my behalf. Amen.

Thursday, March 13

Dear Lord, thank you for loving us so much that you sent your Son to rescue us with His life. Help us love those we touch with the same strength. Amen.

Friday, March 14

Dear Father, help us share Your light. Be with us as we go out each day. Guide us to be used by You in our communities & beyond. Amen.

SATURDAY, MARCH 15

Lord, please guide us through this day with an open heart. Allow us to love all as you love us. Not to judge, but to spread your word and loving nature in every moment of the day. Amen.

SUNDAY, MARCH 16

Father, change us gracefully, so that we are not just giving you part of us, but all of ourselves…To grow in faith, service, and love. Amen.

Lent Prayers 2015

Wednesday, February 18

HOLY FATHER, DIRECT US IN PUTTING ON THE WHOLE ARMOUR OF OUR SPIRITUAL WARFARE TO FIGHT AGAINST ALL WICKEDNESS WITH CONSECRATED FASTINGS, THAT WE MAY BE DEFENDED BY THE POWER OF GOD AND HIS MINISTERING ANGELS, REMEMBERING OUR MORTALITY, THROUGH JESUS CHRIST OUR LORD, AMEN.

Wednesday, February 18

We reinvent ourselves, reposition ourselves, no more "the way we used to do...", all by following the divine direction of our Father, all in love & unity.

This nation, the forces, the elements, they challenge us to BE who & what God has created us to be and many of us are missing it, we're sleeping on it, and before we know it, we have missed this great opportune life our Father has blessed us with...one shot!

Good Morning,

With great enthusiasm, the 2015 Lenten Season begins today (Wed., 02/18), and ends 04/02/15. Today is Ash Wednesday. The ashes are a reminder of our mortality, and without God, we are & can do nothing. We are to humble, abase ourselves before the Throne of God and the Brethren.

Our Bishop, Dr. Young, is reminding us all to give up, sacrifice, abstain from that great faux need, desire, crutch, and expect God to show up.

THURSDAY, FEBRUARY 19

Let us pray, Merciful Father: We confess to you, one another, & the whole company of heaven, that we have sinned by our own fault in thought, word, & deed, by what we have done & by what we have not done. Have mercy on us. Amen.

SATURDAY, FEBRUARY 21

Let us pray: Have mercy on us O God, our negligence in prayer and worship, and our failure to share the faith that is in us, we confess to you. Accomplish in us the work of your salvation. Amen.

SUNDAY, FEBRUARY 22

Let us pray; Compassionate God of times and seasons, You have brought us here again to remind us to study Your Word, for the remembrance of the temptation & suffering of Your Son, and for the contemplation of His Cross. The birds know their seasons; forbid that we be blind to our times. Grant us a penitent blessing, and may no one miss this time of grace. We ask this through Christ our Lord. Amen.

MONDAY, FEBRUARY 23

Let us pray; Father, Our Source of Life, I reach out with joy to grasp Your hand; let me walk more readily in Your ways. Guide me in Your gentle mercy, for left to myself I cannot do Your Will. Amen.

TUESDAY, FEBRUARY 24

Let us pray; Almighty God, who wonderfully created, and more wonderfully restored, the dignity of human nature: Grant us the mind to search ourselves, repent, and humbly take the low position of a servant, so we may share the Divine Life of Your Son, Jesus Christ, who humbled Himself to share our humanity. Amen.

Patient waiting is often the highest way of doing God's Will…Jeremy Collier

WEDNESDAY, FEBRUARY 25

Let us pray; O God, You have created all things by the power of Your Word, and You renew the earth by Your Spirit: Give now the water of life to us who thirst for You, that we may bring forth abundant fruit in Your glorious kingdom; through Jesus Christ our Lord. Amen.

THURSDAY, FEBRUARY 26

Let us pray; Merciful, Most Compassionate God, accompany us on our journey through these penitent days. Renew us in the precious gift of Your Holy Spirit, that we may help the poor, pray for the needy, fast from self-indulgence, and above all, that we may find our treasure in the life of Your Son, our Saviour, Jesus, the Christ. Amen.

FRIDAY, FEBRUARY 27

Let us pray; Father of mercies, and the God of all comfort; You bless us with gifts that sustain our lives; You transform us with the priceless gift of grace. Receive us, and may our fasting, prayer, and works of love be an offering of thanksgiving for all You have done for us, in Christ, our Lord. Amen.

SATURDAY, FEBRUARY 28

Let us pray; Heavenly Father, the fullness of life; help us to be of good courage; to hold fast to that which is good; to render no one evil for evil; to strengthen the fainthearted; to support the weak; to help the afflicted; help us to honor all people; by this we love and serve You, Almighty God, rejoicing in the power of the Holy Ghost. Amen.

SUNDAY, MARCH 01

Let us pray; Most Holy One, Our Father, thank You for this day. Help us as we strive to do Your will as You increase and we decrease. Grant us direction as we draw nearer to Thee in our daily practice to walk upright, and keep your statutes through Christ, our Lord. Amen.

MONDAY, MARCH 02

Let us pray; Father, Most Gracious and Benevolent One, Thank You. Abstaining from cravings, and undesired habits, we remember the days Your Son, Jesus grew closer to that old rugged cross, day-by-day, and step-by-step. We identify and join ourselves with Christ, seeking You, our Father, and Your will. It is here we begin to cry out, united as one, "Answer us, O Lord, Answer us..." Amen.

TUESDAY, MARCH 03

Let us pray; O Compassionate Creator, humbled are we today, before You and our brethren. In the midst of a brewing storm within our members, we ask You to speak to our spirit; command us to reach the other side of this tumultuous sea. We are Your created beings and we submit ourselves to Your will, in Jesus' name, Amen.

WEDNESDAY, MARCH 04

Let us pray; O Heavenly Father, This glorious day we come as one, with one voice, one prayer, one request, to You, The One God..."Answer us, O Lord, Answer us". In Jesus' name, we thank You, Amen.

THURSDAY, MARCH 05

Let us pray; Our Father, Master of Divine Order, and Orchestrator of our times and seasons, thank You for being God. Please, hear our Advocate who pleads our case; forgive us our trespasses; and grant us favor while we strive to do Your will, in Jesus' name. Amen.

FRIDAY, MARCH 06

Let us pray; O Holy, Wonderful God; Prepare me to be a Sanctuary, for You said, "Be ye holy, for I am holy". Our response must be repentance, service, offerings and prayer, by which we recognize our lowliness before the grandeur of the Almighty. Amen.

SATURDAY, MARCH 07

Let us pray; Our Father which art in heaven, this is the day You have made, and in all things we give thanks. Speak to our spirit and mind; bless us with obedience as we humble ourselves. This is our request, for Christ sake, Amen.

SUNDAY, MARCH 08

Let us pray; Father, change us gracefully, so that we are not just giving you part of us, but all of ourselves to grow in faith, service, and love. Amen.

MONDAY, MARCH 09

Let us pray; Precious Lord, please guide us through this day with an open heart. Allow us to love all as You love us; not to judge, but to spread Your Word and loving nature in every moment of the day. Amen.

TUESDAY, MARCH 10

Let us pray; Dear God, Our God, help us to bring under subjection that which hinders us; that which keeps us from staying on task, and restrains us from completing our assignments. We seek to please You, and not to grieve Your Holy Spirit. Help us, O God, help us. Amen.

WEDNESDAY, MARCH 11

Let us pray; Heavenly Father, Thank you for all my yesterdays, and the great gift of today. Let me be truly present for every hello and goodbye, that You may be glorified in each contact I make today. Use us in such a way, that we will need to be in shape just to handle it. Your will. Amen.

THURSDAY, MARCH 12

Let us pray; Most Relevant, Holy One; Thank You for Sound Doctrine, and Spirit-filled, Holy Ghost led Leaders. Help us to be obedient to their teachings. We ask for Divine Favor on this day, that we may exemplify Christ, and not flesh to this dying world. A world whose hope is only in Jesus. Amen.

FRIDAY, MARCH 13

Let us pray; Precious Father, Your love is sweeter than the honey in the honeycomb, and we owe You thanks for loving us the way You do, Thank You. On this glorious day, have pity on us; direct us; keep us; and remind us to stay on task. In Jesus' name, Amen.

SATURDAY, MARCH 14

The highest connection between the mind of man and the Will of God is "Study."

MONDAY, MARCH 16

Let us pray; Father, in Jesus" name, be Thou glorified in all we say and do this day. Help us to think before we speak, and to show compassion to those we are in contact with today. We plead for Your mercy now, that we may tread lightly in those places where we've never been, remembering we are Ambassadors of Your Word and Citizens of Your Kingdom. Let us be a help and not a hinder. Amen.

TUESDAY, MARCH 17

Let us pray; God of our Father's, All Sufficient One; Help us, that we be not passive observers in this walk with Christ, but that we be doers of Your Word; that we actively be our brother's keeper by deed and prayer; and that we passionately be pursuers of lost souls. It is our desire to be effective and productive laborers in Your Harvest. Thank You, for Christ sake, Amen.

WEDNESDAY, MARCH 18

Let us pray; Father of mercies, and the God of all comfort; You bless us with gifts that sustain our lives; You transform us with the priceless gift of grace. Receive us, and may our fasting, prayer, and works of love be an offering of thanksgiving for all You have done for us, in Christ, our Lord. Amen.

THURSDAY, MARCH 19

Let us pray; Thank you, Father for Calvary and the Cross. Amen.

Let us not forget the sacrifice -

But He was hurt because of us; He suffered so. Our wrongdoing wounded and crushed Him. He endured the breaking that made us whole. The injuries He suffered became our healing. We all have wandered off, like shepherdless sheep, scattered by our aimless striving and endless pursuits; The Eternal One laid on Him, this silent sufferer, the sins of us all.

Isaiah 53:5-6 / The Voice

FRIDAY, MARCH 20

Let us pray; Everlasting Father, Soon Coming King, we bless Your Name forever. We honor You; we worship and adore You, we bow down, acknowledging that there is no other god besides Jehovah. We love You, You who rideth the winds, speaks in unconsuming fire, communes with us in that secret place, the holy of holies, the place where mere words cannot express our love and gratitude for You, so, our spirit groans, making intercession for us. Father, receive our thanksgiving, our worship, our prayers with sweet incense from the altar of our hearts to Your Great and Fearful Throne. In Jesus' name, Amen.

Saturday, March 21

Let us pray; Most High God, thank You for this day. In the days when Christ Jesus was in the flesh, He offered prayers and supplications with loud cries and tears to You who was able to save Him from death, and He was heard because of His reverence. Son though He was, He learned obedience from what He suffered; and when He was made perfect, He became the source of Eternal Salvation for all who obey Him. Help us to follow Jesus' example. Amen. Help us, Lord, please, help us. Amen. O God Help us. Amen.

Sunday, March 22

Let us pray; Lord, hear all our prayers. We thank You for all You have given us. Walk with each of us and guide our paths. The earthly trials and worries that weigh us down, help us to turn to You, our help. Let Your light shine on us and in us for the world's hope. Amen.

Monday, March 23

Let us pray; Eternal God, Our Father, glory and honor, dominion and power all belong to You. Thank You for proving Your love for us, not by word only, but indeed. Order our steps; help us to hear and obey Your direction for our days, and prayerfully, productively, patiently wait for Your move, in our midnight. Let our waiting be not one of anxiety, but of confidence that You will show up. In Jesus' name, Amen.

TUESDAY, MARCH 24

Let us pray; Almighty Giver of All Life, Great God of Abraham, Isaac, and Jacob, we worship You. We thank You for allowing us to own every Morning in our lives. By allowing us to take ownership, we have the greatest opportunity to seek Your Will, to obey Your direction, and to give You glory for the successful, productive increase of our blessed day! Just as Jesus took ownership of His days and nights, we follow suit. Amen.

WEDNESDAY, MARCH 25

Let us pray; Dear God, Thank You for comforting us when we are struggling, and loving us when we are down. Encourage us to know You are in control. Amen. 2 Corinthians 1:3 & 4

THURSDAY, MARCH 26

Let us pray; Heavenly Father, thank You for Your Son. Thank You, Jesus for saving all of us, and showing us the way to Your eternal kingdom. Amen.

If any of you are going to walk my path, you are going to have to deny yourself. You will have to take up your cross everyday and follow Me. If you try to avoid danger and risk, then you will lose everything. If you let go of your life, and risk all for my sake, then your life will be rescued, healed, made whole, and full. Luke 9:23 & 24 / Voice

FRIDAY, MARCH 27

Let us pray; Dear Father, Give us the courage to assist those whom we see in trouble & need. Help us to respond just as Jesus would; we are His emissaries. Amen.

SATURDAY, MARCH 28

Let us pray; Kind Father, God of Yesterday, Today, and Forever, we honor, worship, and praise You. We love You and thank You for being mindful of us, Your people. Today, we ask for Your Divine Mercy. Help us to be more conscious of how we treat others. Help us to forgive and release. To receive Your blessings, help us to endure the breaking. Be Thou glorified in this day, Most High Supplier, Our Source. In Jesus' name, Amen.

SUNDAY, MARCH 29

Let us pray; God of our father's, we thank You for keeping us. We are encouraged to take up our cross, drink from the bitter cup, and follow Christ. We bless You for this journey, right here! Amen.

MONDAY, MARCH 30

Let us pray; Father, we adore You and love You. Purposefully we sacrifice time to read Your Word and meditate on the various stages of our Lord's route to the cross. Father, help us to absorb the sacrificial actions, pain, hurt, and bruising Your Son and our Savior took and endured for our sake, not remembering this season only, but always. Thank You Father for Christ being our final unblemished, sacrificial Lamb of God. In Jesus' name, Amen. Hail to Our King!

TUESDAY, MARCH 31

Let us pray; Almighty God, we bless and thank You for who You are, for all You do, and how You do it, even when we don't understand. Your faithfulness has taught us how to trust You, even when we can't see You. We call You, "Keeper of the Covenant"; You who kept us, even when we did not want to be kept, and keeps us still. Help us to defend the faith as good soldiers, and to fight a good fight. We pray that You strengthen the brethren at this very hour, and forever keep us near the cross. In Jesus' name, Amen.

WEDNESDAY, APRIL 01

Let us pray; Our Father, The Great Deity, Most High God, we love You, we bow down before You, we cover our eyes in Your presence because of Your Awesomeness, oh how we yearn to satisfy You! Forgive us our trespasses and help us to seek Your Will for our lives daily. Help, help, help as we deny, deny, deny ourselves, and take up our cross to follow Our Christ. In Jesus' name, Amen.

THURSDAY, APRIL 02

Let us pray; O Master of Divine Order, Conductor of all times and seasons, we bless Your Holy Name. Thank You for giving Your only begotten Son, Jesus, the Christ, who we thank also, for giving His life. Thank You, Jesus for seeing us in that bitter cup. Thank You for every stripe taken for us; for every hit of every nail hammered for us; for every slap and spittle for us; for every tease and taunt for us; for every drop of blood and water for us; for every ache, pain for us; for all grief and sorrow for us; Lord, God, have mercy. We, today, speak the sentiments of the Davidic reply:

What shall I render unto the LORD for all His benefits toward me?

I will take the cup of salvation and call upon the name of the LORD.

I will pay my vows unto the LORD now in the presence of all His people.

I will offer to Thee the sacrifice of thanksgiving and will call upon the name of the LORD. Psalm 116:12-14, 17. Amen.

FRIDAY, APRIL 03

Let us pray; God of all Eternity; Thank You for this day. Refresh us, resurrect us, and restore us for Your glory. Empty us for the Refilling of Your Holy Spirit. Mortify this body that sin may not reign in it any longer. Yesterday is gone; today we begin our task anew; spreading the Gospel everywhere we go, to all we meet. You have given us Your Word to help fortify us for the journey; prayer to continually commune with You for direction; the spirit of watchfulness that the enemy may not come upon us unaware. Have mercy on us. We love You, dear Father, Your people of the Abrahamic Covenant. In Jesus' name we pray, Amen.

SATURDAY, APRIL 04

Let us pray; Compassionate Father, oh, how I love Thee. There is no god besides You. Worshipping You fuels me, it energizes me for the warfare. Early in the morning, You stir my spirit to greet Thee, to engage with You, enthused that I am still in the land of the living, and we are one. O how I love Thee! Order my steps today and help me to release all things into Your hands. Have Your way, in Jesus' name, Amen.

SUNDAY, APRIL 05

Let us pray; Father, Almighty God, Lord of the living and the dead, WE LOVE YOU. We believe that You raised Your Son, and our Savior from the dead approximately over 2000 years ago! THANK YOU, JESUS,! ON THIS RESURRECTION MORNING FOR GETTING UP! We owe it all to You. Thank You, Father for Jesus bringing about reconciliation between us and You. All power is given unto Him in heaven and in earth. Thank You, Jesus for being with us always, even unto the end of the world. ALL HAIL KING JESUS! ALL HAIL EMMANUEL! AMEN.

MONDAY, APRIL 06

Let us pray; Father, in Jesus' name, we thank You for the sun, moon, and the stars; the planets in and outside of our solar system; we thank You for the ozone layer, the plants that help give us oxygen and show their beauty; we thank You for our jobs, homes, food, clothing, finances, clean water, family and friends. We thank You for FAVOR! But, most of all, we thank You for Your Son, Jesus Christ, the gift of the Holy Ghost, and the plan of Salvation. Amen.

TUESDAY, APRIL 07

Let us pray; Gracious Father, thank You for another glorious day. On this day, we ask You to walk with us, and talk with us. Give us direction in the various matters we're faced with. Help us to make the right choices and decisions today. Let us seek Your input in all we do today, and not to take our commune with You lightly. Have mercy on us, renew our strength naturally and spiritually. In Jesus' name we pray, Amen.

WEDNESDAY, APRIL 08

Let us pray; Secure Father, Keeper of my soul, thank You for revealing who we are through Your Word. Not just who we are in the flesh, but much more who we are in Christ. Paul said, "But I see another law in my members, warring against the law of my mind, and bringing me into captivity to the law of sin which is in my members" (Romans 7:23 KJV). But Your Word gives us a way of escape, "Casting down imaginations, and every high thing that exalteth itself against the knowledge of God, and bringing into captivity every thought to the obedience of Christ;" (2 Corinthians 10:5 KJV). God, have mercy on us, and continue to give us grace this blessed day. Amen.

THURSDAY, APRIL 09

Let us pray; O Great Sustainer; Almighty Supporter; My Tower of Strength; I need Thee, O how I need Thee, every, every, every hour, I need Thee, bless me now, my Savior, I come to Thee. For where else shall I go? Only You know and understand the obstacles I face, but I get peace knowing that though the weapon may form, it will not prosper. Again, I ask for Your direction in these matters. I've made enough bad decisions, and wrong choices, but in this, right here, I come to You. Have mercy, Dear Lord. Please, extend to me Your Divine Grace for the journey. In Jesus' name, Amen.

FRIDAY, APRIL 10

Let us pray; Kind Father, we magnify You, we glorify You, we honor You, we bow down and worship You. Thank You for being God. This morning, we just want to thank You for all You are to us; Comforter, Supplier; Source; Life; Keeper; Deliverer; Sustainer; Counselor; and everything else in between. Through Jesus' name we've seen You turn our blunders into blessings, and we thank You for the lessons we've learned. Have mercy on us. Amen.

SATURDAY, APRIL 11

Let us pray; Eternal Spirit, Sovereign Creator; You are our all and all, and we thank You. Have mercy on us, forgive us for all we are guilty of that was not pleasing in Your sight. We pray for political leaders all over this world, and especially for our leaders here in these United States of America. We pray for our spiritual leaders. These are those whose prayers to You cause Presidents to sign laws into effect; pardon death penalties; speak words of wisdom at peace conferences, and so much more. Strengthen and encourage them. Help us who follow them to be a help, and not a hinder. We pray for the brethren. Dry tears, encourage hearts, meet needs, bind the hand of the enemy, restore what has been taken, return their hearts back to You, and have mercy on us. In Jesus' name, Amen.

SUNDAY, APRIL 12

Let us pray; Heavenly Father, this is a good day, and we thank you for it. Your bountiful blessings are more than we deserve, but we are so grateful that You care. We love You, Father. We thank You for the all-powerful name of Jesus, Amen.

Monday, April 13

Let us pray; O Benevolent One, we greet Thee on the cusp of this great day. We look forward to mighty acts, miracles, and unexpected expectations. What a mighty God we serve. Now, Father, we pray for our children. Innocently, too many are leaving us because of improper supervision by irresponsible adults, most of the time. Have mercy on us. Father, assign guardian angels for our children who will escort them to and fro, let the children follow their intuition although they may not understand. Stir the guardians to attend a house of prayer, hear their spiritual leaders, pray and be more watchful, seek Your direction, and having the Holy Spirit, activate their discernment. We speak life for our children, in Jesus' name, Amen.

Tuesday, April 14

Let us pray; Heavenly Father, Order our steps this day. We thank You for hearing and answering our petitions. Thank You for this great privilege, to be able to openly and privately communicate with You through this vehicle of prayer. Help us not to take lightly our gathering together in houses of prayer to worship in Jesus' name, but to see this great gift given us here in this country, and to pray for others who are forbidden to do so in other countries. This stands true also for reading and possessing Your written Word. Thank You, our Father. Amen.

Wednesday, April 15

Let us pray; Most Holy Father, we come in a quiet place, at a quiet hour, with a quiet heart to offer You a sacrifice of sincere gratitude. You are our peacemaker, and our peacekeeper. Thank You, Almighty Shalom. Your secret place is our prayer room, where You soothe our broken spirits, catch our dense hot tears, and our rivers of weeping. You dismiss our fears of yesterday and encourage our hopes of today. We love You for Your warm, full embrace. For when words have failed us, and we have ended and sealed our prayer with Selah, when worship and praise, glory and honor have been raised for the sake of Christ, prepare our hearts and spirits to come before You again in prayer, all through this day. In Jesus' name, Amen/Selah.

THURSDAY, APRIL 16

Let us pray; Almighty God, how wonderful it is to greet You here today, in the land of the living. Thank You for another day. Father retrain our ears to hear Your still, sweet voice as it directs and communes with us. Let us not be distracted by the foolishness of the enemy. Help us to polarize our thoughts before they become living words. Help us to stay on task and complete our assignment this day, all to Your glory. We look forward to meeting You again in prayer momentarily, with our hearts stayed on You. We bless You now, in Jesus' name, Amen.

FRIDAY, APRIL 17

Let us pray; O Lord, our Lord, Most Holy God, we come this morning with heads bowed, hearts humbled, and thanks on our lips. Your love for us is immeasurable and cannot be compared to any other. We love You because You first loved us. We thank You for loving us. Help us to cry out to You for direction as we lay on the altar those things which causes us to feel unaccomplished. Father, draw us nearer to You by revealing to us daily Your plans for us. Bless us throughout this day and use us for Your glory. In Jesus' name, Amen.

SATURDAY, APRIL 18

Let us pray; O Great Healer, Our Chief Surgeon; we give You thanks for life this morning. We ask that You lay Your healing hands on our natural bodies. Speak wellness and wholeness from the crown of our heads to the soles of our feet, from the inside out. Restore excellent health where there is a decline; we call for the Elders, anointing ourselves with the blessed oil, praying the prayer of faith, and knowing You will restore. In Jesus' name we pray, Amen.

SUNDAY, APRIL 19

Let us pray; Father, my hope is built on nothing less than Jesus' blood and righteousness; I dare not trust the sweetest frame, But wholly lean on Jesus' name. On Christ, the solid Rock, I stand; All other ground is sinking sand. O Immutable One, this is my creed and oath. Faithful is Your name. And, when I've done all to stand, Father, help me to stand therefore, knowing You will. In Jesus' name, Amen/Selah.

MONDAY, APRIL 20

Let us pray; Everlasting Father, Faithful and True; thank You this morning for life, health, and a mind to serve You. We owe You praise for Your kindness toward us. Thank You for Divine Protection, keeping us from dangers seen and unseen. Bless us to yield to Your will this day; our members are Your tools to do Your bidding. Let us seize the opportunity to speak life and offer Christ to some lost soul today. In Jesus' name, Amen.

TUESDAY, APRIL 21

Let us pray; Most Holy Father, we humbly bow before You, thanking You for all You do for us. Thank You for the lost souls we minister to and look forward to You giving the increase. We ask for mercy. Forgive us our trespasses as we forgive others. Father, search our hearts, reveal our hidden selves, but not hidden to You. We place these things on the altar before You, asking for deliverance. Make and mold us, help us to willingly yield to Your masterful potter's hand.

PATRICIA A. COHEN

We love You and appreciate Your chastening, showing Your love for us. We look forward to a better us. In Jesus' name, Amen/Selah.

WEDNESDAY, APRIL 22

Let us pray; Merciful Father, today we face great challenges that will increase our faith. Challenges that will reaffirm that You are God, and besides You, there is no other. Challenges to reaffirm You can do all things, and that with You, we too, can do all things through Christ who strengthens us. Bless us and our dwelling place. We love You, and adore You. Thank You for answering our prayers, in Jesus' name, Amen.

THURSDAY, APRIL 23

Let us pray; Our Supreme Instructor, Our Commander-in-Chief; we bless Your holy name. Glorious are the days You've given us. Marvelous are the blessings You've bestowed upon us. Wondrous are Your ways which bring pleasure to our lives. We thank You for being the love of our lives. O my God! Cover our military troops everywhere. Help them to be strong, and to trust You most. Grant favor to America's militia in their duties, and bring them home alive, safe and sound. Above all, Father, let Your will be done. We seal this prayer in Jesus' name, Amen/Selah.

FRIDAY, APRIL 24

Let us pray; With all the activities of all of our limbs, we give You praise; Almighty God of mercy, and Father of all comfort, great is Thy faithfulness, morning by morning, new mercies we see! Selah. Thank You, O Gracious One. On the cusp of a new day, direct our steps with Your purpose to be fulfilled. Bless our commune with You all through this day as we listen to what You have to say to us. Thank You for divine direction. Bless the brethren as we pray for one another, united with one voice, for one purpose, unto You we give thanks, our One God. In Jesus' name, Amen/Selah.

SATURDAY, APRIL 25

Let us pray; Master, Keeper, Deliverer, Father; we come this morning with joy in the spirit of worship. Joy because You have done what You said You would. Your Word says, *"God is not a man, that He should lie; neither the son of man, that He should repent: hath He said, and shall He not do it? or hath He spoken, and shall He not make it good?" Great God that You are, we thank You for Your goodness, for Your mercy, and there is just something about Your grace! Thank You, Father, thank You. Guide us today. Sealing and declaring in Jesus' name, Amen/Selah.

*Numbers 23:19

(Sick & Shut-in Prayer)

Father, in Jesus' name; we come in unison thanking You for all being well by our faith. We are lifting before Your throne of grace for healing naturally and spiritually, our Bishop Deloris Young, Elder Joseph Young, Sr., Sis. Sandra Baldwin, Lady Joyce Terrell, Min. Will Latham, Sis. Rose Ragland, Sis. Marie Blake, Bro. Nathaniel Dickerson, Sis. Charlesetta Singleton, Sis. Canesha Owens, Bishop Wesley Braziel, Bishop Philip Cargile, Sr., Sis. Emma Spearman, Evang. Patricia Cohen, Sis. Rosa Cargile, Sis. Verna Williams, Sis. Alfreda, Bro. Walker; the families of the five deceased nursing students in the I-16 accident this week: Emily Clark; McKay Pittman; Caitlyn Baggett; Morgan Bass, and Abbie Deloach, and the two injured, Brittney McDaniel, and Megan Richards. We submit also to You the truck driver, John Wayne Johnson, and unknown and unnamed others. We call upon You, the Father of mercy, and the God of all Comfort. Do what You do best, BE GOD. Amen.

SUNDAY, APRIL 26

Let us pray; Thank You, Father for the closing of this day. Amen.

MONDAY, APRIL 27

Let us pray; O Awesome Wonder, Grantor of all Gifts; thank You for every soul saved, everybody healed, every mind changed toward You, every debt cancelled, every financial increase, every job promotion, every monumental miracle, every blessed favor, every heart healed, and everything governed and ordained by You for us. Help us not to take our daily blessings for granted, no matter how used we get to receiving them. Help us to remember to always honor and thank You for these great blessings You bestow upon us. O Great Wonder, how we love You. O how bright is the sun/Son after the storm! Bless us this beautiful day, in Jesus' name, Amen/Selah.

TUESDAY, APRIL 28

Let us pray; Great Redeemer, O Holy One of Israel; thank You for sound doctrine and those who propagate Your Word. Bless Your Leaders who are spreading the Word to all with equal amounts of wise warning and instruction, so that, at the final judgment, they will be able to present everyone to You, the Creator fully MATURE because of what Jesus Christ, our Liberating King, has done. Strengthen us, Your Sons to be stable, rooted and grounded, not following wayward others. Let us search the scriptures, praying for *the Spirit to search all things so that our spiritual leaders, as well as ourselves will be found blameless on **the Day of Visitation. Thank You for answering our prayers and granting our requests. Nevertheless, not our will, but Thine be done. We humbly receive Your direction, submit and seal this prayer in Jesus' name, Amen/Selah.

* 1 Corinthians 2:10
** 1 Peter 2:12

WEDNESDAY, APRIL 29

Let us pray; Most Gracious and Kind Father; we thank You this beautiful morning for Your mighty acts and kindness toward us. We humbly lay ourselves at Your Feet of Mercy and Your Throne of Grace as we go through the trials of our faith. We will bless You at all times, in all things. Strengthen the weak, heal the afflicted, encourage the downtrodden, make whole the broken, restore the port in the storm, and renew the joy. Thank You for Your saving Son, Jesus, who sits on the right hand of Your Power, intercepting and pleading our causes. Bless this day, in Jesus' name, Amen/Selah.

THURSDAY, APRIL 30

Let us pray; Almighty Keeper of our heart, mind, and spirit; You are the brightness of our morning, and the lullaby of our midnight. There is none like You. Father, You direct and guide us every step of this journey, because we seek You to do so. We trust You all the way. Thank You for Your Divine Protection. We awake on the verge of a new day, anxious to greet and speak with You about our love for You, and our cares. Help us to hear and obey Your soothing voice of comfort and direction. Waiting to hear from You is as a woman waiting on her lover to come calling. We love You with every fiber of our being. Keep our mind stayed and focused on You as we flow through this blessed day. In Jesus' name, Lord, we honor You, Amen.

FRIDAY, MAY 01

Let us pray; O Great Jehovah, we thank You for strength, courage, joy, peace, love, direction, stability, and a mind to serve You. Thank You for the wisdom of our seasons through the knowledge of Your Word. Thank You for great revelations through our victories in Christ Jesus. We love how You love us. Keep us in that secret place, and let not our feet to be moved. We thank You for the marvelous wonders that will manifest before our very eyes today. To God be the glory. For Christ sake, in Jesus' name, Amen/Selah

SATURDAY, MAY 02

Let us pray; Our Father, this is a good day. We will joyously go out and declare the Word of the Lord. We will make known Your deeds among the people. We will seize the opportunity to compel some dying soul to come to Christ. We will speak words of encouragment, life to the brethren. This is the day we will lift Your name higher. We will carry ourselves with the awareness that we are in Your presence, and the fruit we produce today will be for Your glory; all men will see we are Your people. We ask for direction today and not to take this day lightly; for granted. We thank You, love and bless Your name. For Christ sake, Amen/Selah.

SUNDAY, MAY 03

Let us pray; Most Holy and Wise God, we thank You for this day and allowing us to live to enjoy it. Thank You for the fellowship of the brethren, and Your love which is spread abroad. Thank You for the many messages You've given us today. Thank You for Your Angels that You have used to speak words of life to us, Your people. Bless these angels, keep them healed, meet every need, increase finances, direct these angels, give them great revelations, manifest their dreams, and bring to past their visions, for Christ sake and the glory of God. Help us to receive, share, and obey Your instructions for life and living. In Jesus' name, Amen/Selah.

MONDAY, MAY 04

Let us pray; Most Generous One, God of Our Fathers, we thank You for this new day, and the multiplicity of awesome gifts this day holds for us. Help us not to miss the gifts of what we need by looking only for the gifts of what we want, have mercy on us. Go before us on this day, make the pathway straight. Have Your divine way in our lives. It is with great joy that we serve You, Almighty Giver of all life. Bless our families and loved ones. Help us to pray for them that spitefully try to use us. Convict their spirits, and turn their hearts to You. Be Thou glorified in all things, in Jesus' name, Amen/Selah.

TUESDAY, MAY 05

Let us pray; All Sufficient One, Great is Thy faithfulness! Thank You for Your healing power. Thank You for going to the root of the issue, arresting and killing it, so it will return no more. We thank You for the doctors and their staff, and the knowledge You've given them, but our healing comes from You. Thank You, Our Father. For whatever is going on, we declare and decree, we will take up our bed and WALK! The gifts You have blessed us with shall bear GOOD fruit, and will not die at any pity party, with tears served as our drink, and sad stories served as the main course! THIS IS THE DAY THAT THE LORD HATH MADE, WE WILL REJOICE, AND BE GLAD IN IT! Father, in Jesus' name, this day is already blessed. Amen/Selah.

MY DECLARATION FOR TODAY:
I CONFESS, DECLARE AND DECREE,
AS THE MIGHTY SOLDIER THAT I AM,
I WILL NOT GO BY WHAT I SEE,
I WILL NOT RECEIVE EVERYTHING I HEAR,
I WILL BELIEVE WHAT GOD HAS SAID,
AND I WILL SPEAK GOD'S WORD,
UNTIL I SEE IT AND LAY HOLD ON IT!
GOD HAS NOT GIVEN ME THE SPIRIT OF FEAR.
SO, TO THIS CHALLENGE OF MY FAITH, I SAY,
I AIN'T SCARED, I BELIEVE GOD!

WEDNESDAY, MAY 06

Let us pray; Great Sender of the Comforter, we greet You this marvelous, beautiful day. Thank You in all things; we are, and ever will be grateful to You. Today, we intercede for the incarcerated. Have mercy on those who are there innocently. Speak to the spirits of them who have authority over the release and care of them, and soften their hearts to show compassion. Let the truth be known, and we will accept it. Now, Kind Father, have pity on those who are guilty, and give them repentant hearts. We plead with You to move on the authorities to take another look at these cases where the punishment does not fit the crime, readjust the sentence, consider time already served, and bless the judge who rules in their favor. Let these men and women go and sin no more, letting these things be a testimony of Your great magnanimous mercy and glorious grace. We all have come short, somewhere, and if it wasn't for Your grace and mercy only You know where we'd be. Have Your way, in Jesus' name we submit these requests for Your glory, Amen/Selah.

THURSDAY, MAY 07

Let us pray; Saver of all Souls, Giver of The Holy Ghost; thank You for another fruitful day. As we go through our day let us see the beauty of Your creations, and give thanks. We thank You for souls being saved, hearts changed, spirits yield, changes embraced, bodies healed, finances released and increased, needs met, dreams coming to past, visions manifested, the harvest being plentiful, and the laborers being added to the fold. With this day already being blessed, we glorify You for it. In Thy Son, Jesus' name, Amen/Selah.

FRIDAY, MAY 08

Let us pray; Father, it is refreshing to know You are always there for us at the breaking of each new day. In all things, we give You thanks, praise, and honor. Today, we pray for guidance for our children. Although some are of adult age, and they think they know their own direction, we ask You to speak to their hearts. We as parents, have done all we can, and we have given them back to You. We trust You with them, because they are Yours. Reveal Yourself to them. Stir up the gifts on the inside of them. We pray for "greater" for them. Help us be the examples You've ordained. Show us how to communicate with our children, and teach us to listen to what they are saying. Let our discernment be activated for their sake. We ask for divine protection for them. Let Your angels escort them to-and-from various destinations. Use them for Your glory, in Jesus' name, Amen/Selah.

SATURDAY, MAY 09

Let us pray; Father, this morning we sing Your praises; O taste and see that the Lord is good; You have fought and won our battles, You have given us the victory, You have delivered into our hands the land, the riches, and the goods. Above all, You have given us a peace of mind wherein we are able to meditate on all the great and mighty acts You've performed for us. Bless Your mighty name. Thank You for every mother here and gone. We thank You for their loving, nurturing qualities used to raise not only their children, but the love shown to so many others not of their blood. Thank You for the memories, the laughter and tears, the chastising, the sharp eye and firm hand, the teachings, the learned value of their struggles, and the power of their victories for the family! Now we know. Bless us with our families, as we keep You first in all things. In Jesus' name, Amen/Selah.

SUNDAY, MAY 10

Let us pray; O Holy Father, we are overflowing with joy, thanking You for another glorious day. Our joy is from knowing You are God. We trust Your direction for our very lives. Thank You for giving us Your best, Your Son, Jesus as a ransom for us, Your children. We love You. Have Your way, in Jesus' name, Amen/Selah.

MONDAY, MAY 11

Let us pray; Father, in Jesus' name we thank You for another absolutely wonderful day. The plans You've made for us today are well worth the work. Help us to see and understand the worth of being able to exert the energy to achieve the desires of our hearts. Your Word says, *Delight thyself also in the LORD: and He shall give thee the desires of thine heart. Also, Your Word reminds us, ** For as the body without the spirit is dead, so faith without works is dead also. We thank You for our jobs, natural and spiritual, and our abundant increase through the faith and working of it. For the sake of increase, Amen/Selah.

*Psalm 37:4
**James 2:26

TUESDAY, MAY 12

Let us pray; Father, we are so grateful for knowing You. Knowing You as our Father and our God is comfort enough to make it through this day. Knowing we can call on You at anytime, for anything, anywhere brings joy, excitement, peace, and such relief it astounds us. Thank You for answering our call. In Jesus' name, Amen/Selah.

WEDNESDAY, MAY 13

Let us pray; Father, we greet You and thank You for the coolness of this great day. We are so grateful. As we pass others unknown to us, let us be aware of our countenance and our tone of voice, remembering, we are Your Ambassadors, and some people's only Bible. Let us offer Christ to those outside of the Ark of Safety, and encourage the brethren to stay fast in the faith, without controversy. This is for the glory of God. Bless our journey today, in Jesus' name, Amen/Selah.

THURSDAY, MAY 14

Let us pray; O Thou Great Jehovah, we honor You. We acknowledge You in all of Your glory. Guide us today. Help us to stay in constant dialogue with You. There is peace in knowing You hear us, and You will answer. Counsel is needed today for every circumstance and situation. Lead us in every choice and decision today, that there will be no regrets. Help us to patiently wait on You. We declare and decree with Your help, the enemy will not force our hand. In Jesus' name, Amen/Selah.

FRIDAY, MAY 15

Let us pray; Most Holy and Righteous Father, it is with great joy that we present ourselves before You today. Salvation to our God which sitteth upon the throne, and unto the Lamb. We have no complaints, just extreme gratitude for all You've done. Your kindness is amazing. Have mercy on us this day. We thank You for Your Son, whose name is called Faithful and True. We thank You for His vesture dipped in blood as He goes to war for us. We bow before Your throne as all of heaven bears witness, and earth looks on as Your blessings flow with us today. Amen: Blessing, and glory, and wisdom, and thanksgiving, and honour, and power, and might, be unto our God for ever and ever. Amen/Selah.

SATURDAY, MAY 16

Let us pray; Father, at the close of this day, as we enter into the night, betwixt and between these hours where the day slowly becomes dusk, the cool moisture in the air becomes dew, the aches and pains of this day become a testimony that we are still here. The lights still function, the water is still running, the phones still ring, food is in our refrigerators, clothes are in our closets, the houses/apartments and cars are still in our possession. We have peace knowing all of this is because we asked, and You gave. The glory belongs to You, and we are so grateful. We owe all to You. You are, and forever will be our only God. In Jesus' name, Amen/Selah.

SUNDAY, MAY 17

Let us pray; Most Majestic God, we thank You for this day, this is a good day. We thank You for Your mercy and Your grace. We so enjoy being in Your presence, and having You dwell among us. Bless those we've fellowshipped with today. Make us one. Help us not to be led or guided by our emotions, but to place our feelings under the Blood of Christ, that we may be clear, and precise with our remarks, choices, and decisions. Activate our discernment, give us more compassion for our brothers and sisters. Help us to see our own shortcomings before glorying in another's stumbling. Draw us nearer to Thee, in Jesus' name, we ask for Your help, Amen/Selah.

MONDAY, MAY 18

Let us pray; Blessed Father, You, and You alone are God. Thank You for this day. Thank You for answering our prayers. Go before us that we may accomplish Your will on this day. Let us hear and obey when You speak. Help us to be kind to one another. Remember the brethren in a special way. This day is already blessed, in Jesus' name we pray, Amen/Selah.

TUESDAY, MAY 19

Let us pray; In a place where each day presents so many uncertainties, one thing is undeniable and sure...GOD IS IN CONTROL. Thank You for Your Word being fool-proof, tried-and-true. Father, in Jesus' mighty name, we greet You with grateful hearts. We anticipate, and expect great and marvelous wonders, acts of unusual kindness toward us, Your people this day. Bless us to be a blessing, help us to help somebody else, lift us so that we may be a lifter. Give us an attitude adjustment on life and living so that we don't miss our many blessings. Give safe travel and divine protection to those who are out and abroad. With this day being already blessed, we love You, and thank You for Your divine mercy and grace, Amen/Selah.

WEDNESDAY, MAY 20

Let us pray; Merciful One, we thank You for life. Strengthen our bodies. Renew our minds. Help us to do that which we know is right. Thank You for continually opening doors, supplying our needs, directing our paths, giving us favor. The joy of the Lord is our strength, in Jesus' name, Amen/Selah.

THURSDAY, MAY 21

Let us pray; Gracious Father, we thank You for the Power of the Holy Ghost, the Comforter which You sent back to us, to help us on this journey. As we approach Pentecost Sunday, help us to see and understand the value of this great gift and how to use it by Your direction for Your glory. Oh, the joy that floods our souls. Thank You, Lord for the fulfillment of Your Promise, in Jesus' name, Amen/Selah.

FRIDAY, MAY 22

Let us pray; Our Father, we sincerely thank You for all the men and women who have given their lives defending our country and its citizens. We thank You and pray for them who are still with us, and have sacrificed limbs, senses, families, and even peace of mind. We pray for those who continue to defend our great nation. We pray for all the leaders of the branches of our armed forces, that they will seek direction from You before making decisions regarding our nation. Lead them to seek sound spiritual guidance for Your people's sake. Comfort the families and give them Your peace, in Jesus' name, Amen/Selah.

SATURDAY, MAY 23

Let us pray; Kind Father, we thank You for this most profitable and glorious day. Profitable, because we've gained and not lost. Glorious, because we've celebrated and are not ashamed. Thank You for Your Angels which keep watch and complete assignments for You and us. The evening and the morning are blessed and we thank You, in Jesus' name, Amen/Selah.

SUNDAY, MAY 24

Let us pray; O Great Keeper of the Promise; Thank You, thank You, thank You. We are so grateful to You, Father for sending us the Gift of the Holy Ghost, the Comforter to lead and guide us into all truth. Help us to keep our temples clean daily, so that the Holy Spirit may dwell there. Help us to keep our thoughts, words, tones, actions, and ways clean so we may receive its teachings, understanding, and wisdom that we may exemplify Christ. Let us not remember this today only, but everyday, that we may live according to Your Word, Holy. Glorious, O Glorious day, in Jesus' name, continue to keep us, Amen/Selah.

TUESDAY, MAY 26

Let us pray; Most Heavenly Father, Keeper of our minds, and Restorer of our strength; Thank You for Your kindness toward us. Your favor is as a fresh wind blowing on the nape of our necks in the heat of the day. Doing Your Will and showing kindness to our fellowman is how we say thanks for all You've done for us, many things You've done and changed in our favor we may never even know. You're just that kind of God. Bless those who are struggling financially, keep those who are faltering, console the bereaved, counsel those who are in disarray, and remember the rest of us in our needs. Provider that You are, we trust You for all things, even our secret requests. In Jesus' name we seal this prayer, Amen/Selah.

WEDNESDAY, MAY 27

My brothers and sisters, I have enjoyed sharing prayer times with you. Certainly, our Great, Majestic God is good. My desire is that our prayer lives will continue to increase, even as our spiritual lives abound. I bid you health, wealth, riches, liberty, peace, and love, in Jesus's name. I love you all.

Chapter Two

LENT PRAYERS 2016

TUESDAY, FEBRUARY 09

Lent is the season of penance and prayer before Easter. Because Easter is a moveable feast, the date of Easter changes every year, which means that the dates when Lent begins and ends do, too.

Fasting, as well as prayer and almsgiving is a functional and participatory part of Lent. During Lent, you are asked to choose an item (usually a food) to give up while submitting to God. This sacrifice assists bringing your whole man (spirit, soul, and body) back into reconciliation with the Father and His Divine Will.

Let us draw nigh unto Christ. Let us focus on submission as we take up our cross and follow Jesus in yielding to The Father's Most Holy Will for our lives, our churches, and our communities.

WEDNESDAY, FEBRUARY 10

Let us pray: Father, in Jesus' name, we cry loud for mercy. Forgive us our transgressions of words and deeds, as we forgive and release those who have offended us. Grant to us, O Lord, to put on the whole armour of God in our Christian warfare with holy fastings; that we who are fighting against spiritual wickedness may be defended by the power of abstinence, through Christ Our Lord, Amen.

THURSDAY, FEBRUARY 11

Let us pray; Most Holy and Righteous Father, we come with humbled hearts, quieted spirits, and thanksgiving upon our lips. Direct us in Thy way, keep us on Thy path, that we may lead others to You, in Jesus' name, Amen.

FRIDAY, FEBRUARY 12

Let us pray; Gracious Father, this is the day You have made, we will rejoice and be glad in it. This day is hallowed because of Thy Word; Thy Word is pure, it is sure, it is just, it is correct, and it is full of mercy and compassion. We will embrace this day by purposefully being Your witness in word and deed to some needy soul. We thank you for the blessings of sharing, in Jesus' name, Amen.

SATURDAY, FEBRUARY 13

Let us pray: Father, in Jesus' name, we cry loud for mercy. Forgive us our transgressions of words and deeds, as we forgive and release those who have offended us. Grant to us, O Lord, to put on the whole armour of God in our Christian warfare with holy fastings; that we who are fighting against spiritual wickedness may be defended by the power of abstinence, through Christ Our Lord, Amen.

SUNDAY, FEBRUARY 14

Let us pray; All Mighty God, great and marvelous are Thy works! Have mercy on us this morning. Search our hearts, sanctify our whole man. Purge us with hyssop, and we shall be clean: wash us, and we shall be whiter than snow. Have Your way this day, and we thank You, in Jesus' name, Amen.

MONDAY, FEBRUARY 15

Let us pray; Dear Father, we thank and bless You for this day. Direct our path, polarize our thoughts, and let our compassion abound for those who are without the gate. Grant us mercy and grace, in Jesus' name, Amen.

TUESDAY, FEBRUARY 16

Let us pray; Gracious and Caring Father, out of the abundance of Your mercy hide us from the enemies who lay traps for our souls. Out of Your mouth has been spoken a perpetual word that forbids any to go beyond Your indelible mark! For the boundaries are set, You are our defense, and for this, we give You praise. Humbly we thank You in Jesus' name, Amen.

WEDNESDAY, FEBRUARY 17

Let us pray; O Merciful Father, help us to submit ourselves to mind the things of the Spirit, and to refuse the things of the flesh; no more to be carnal minded, but laying hold of the weapons of our warfare, casting down imaginations, and every high thing that exalteth itself against the knowledge of God, bringing into captivity every thought to the obedience of Christ who gives us the victory; for our warfare is in heavenly places. We yield our members to You, in Jesus' name, Amen.

THURSDAY, FEBRUARY 18

Let us pray; To The Only Wise God, we come saying, "Thank You" this morning for all You've done. We pray now for those who are lost, lead them out of the wilderness; if they are hungry, feed them with Your Word; naked, clothe them; despondent, lift them; poor, make rich with Your Spirit; discontent, fill them with Your joy. Then Lord, remember us who are trying daily to reach the masses. Help us to not be weary in well doing. In Jesus's name, Amen.

FRIDAY, FEBRUARY 19

Let us pray; Everlasting Father, Awesome Wonder, great and mighty are Thy works. We rest in You, knowing all things are working for our good; we love you and are called according to Your purpose. We implore You to have Your divine way in our lives. You are always right; we humbly submit ourselves to Your Will and Your Way. In Jesus' name, Amen.

Saturday, February 20

Let us pray; Our Father, it is with exceeding joy that we rise this morning, thanking You for peace of mind; a desire to serve You, the brethren, and to help those in need. We cannot draw closer to You by serving only our own household, but with the Spirit of Christ we serve our fellowman with love and kindness, that they may see You in our lives. Today, we will intentionally help someone in need by Your leading, that You may be glorified, the body of Christ edified, and servanthood increased. In Jesus' name, Amen.

Sunday, February 21

Let us pray; All Knowing, All Powerful, and Ever Present God; Our souls delight in the fatness of Your Word and we are satisfied with the abundance of Your goodness. We are complete today according to Your Word and by the steadfastness of our faith. All things are because of You, and we praise You for it. We look to You for our help and that right swiftly; for Your love for Your children never waxes cold. We thank You, in Jesus' name, Amen.

Monday, February 22

Let us pray; Praise You, O God, from Whom all blessings flow. We lift before You our body of government; from our President, Mr. Obama, down to every volunteer and civil servant. Speak to their hearts that they may obey Your direction. Remember the Saints, believers, and all foreigners who dwell in this nation as Statutes, Regulations, Ordinances and Common Laws made by city, county, state and federal governments are passed and set. We pray for our government official's families that there might be peace in the homes. Lead them for Your people's sake. In Jesus' name, Amen.

TUESDAY, FEBRUARY 23

Let us pray; Heavenly Father, it is with gladness of heart that we eagerly serve You. Have mercy on us. Help us in the midst of our troubles, teach us to encourage ourselves, help us to remember the many times You have moved mountains and people, stretched finances and kept back the devourer, made and allowed changes in us and in our lives that we ourselves sometimes didn't understand; for our sakes. We thank You for lifting. We honor You, True and Faithful, Lover of our souls. In Jesus" name, Amen.

WEDNESDAY, FEBRUARY 24

Let us pray; O Divine Creator, We thank You this morning for all that you have done. We pray today for the men of God, the priests of our households. Spiritually strengthen them and increase might. For those who know You in the pardon of their sins, but have gotten out of place, restore the mind of Christ that they may take their rightful place once again. Remove the spirit of fear and slothfulness. Let them see their contrary ways, unbridled lusts, and humiliating bad habits. Let the spirit of shame cross the threshold of their lives that they may see themselves and turn back to You. Father, have mercy on them. For those men who just don't know what to do, we ask that you give them a mind to seek You for direction, do not let them be satisfied to be as other men, but to be the man You have called them to be. Stir up the gift(s) within. Have Your divine way, in Jesus' name, Amen.

THURSDAY, FEBRUARY 25

Let us pray; Heavenly Father, Great is Thy Faithfulness toward us! We thank You for every personalized blessing of every brand new day. Help us to yield to Your direction this day. We deny the flesh and invite Your Holy Spirit to sup with us. For Christ's sake, in Jesus' name, Amen.

FRIDAY, FEBRUARY 26

Let us pray; Blessed be the name of the Lord who is the Light of all lights and dispels all darkness; Whose Truth reveals all lies, and Whose spoken; even uttered Word, by unwavering faith, maketh the blind see, the lame walk, dumb talk, deaf hear, lost found, poor rich, and He maketh the obedient not keep company with the disobedient; that our sacrifice of praise; the fruit of our lips, may be acceptable as a sweet smelling savour to the Father. Lord, this day, help us to remember who we are and whose we are; thereby walking worthy of the vocation wherein we are called. Now be all glory and power, dominion and majesty to the Lord God, our Saviour, through Jesus Christ for time and times to come, Amen.

SATURDAY, FEBRUARY 27

Let us pray; Merciful Father, thank You for life on this new and glorious morning. We pray for those who are less fortunate than us. Thank You for others You have placed in our lives to be a blessing and to bless. Lead and guide us in our journey today, in Jesus' name, Amen.

SUNDAY, FEBRUARY 28

Let us pray; Compassionate and Most Merciful Father, we thank You for being so good to us; for while we were yet in our sins, You gave Your only begotten Son to die for us. Today, we commit into Your hands every situation we have no control over, and that situation we do have some say in, we seek Your direction before we utter a word. We glorify You this day in both life and death. In Jesus's name, Amen.

MONDAY, FEBRUARY 29

Let us pray; Father, it is with much gratitude that we approach Your Throne of Mercy today; grateful for Your mercy and grace, love and kindness, compassion and understanding, correction and direction, for life and another opportunity to witness for you in this life. Have Your way, in Jesus' name, Amen.

TUESDAY, MARCH 01

Let us pray; Great is Thy Faithfulness, O Lord, unto us, Your people. The extremes, the lengths, the depths, the heights, and the breadth that You go to bless us, Your people again, and again, and again are immeasurable! Your mercy and grace cause us to ask and answer, What shall I render unto the LORD for all His benefits toward me? I will take the cup of salvation, and call upon the name of the LORD. I will pay my vows unto the LORD now in the presence of all His people. Father, we owe You, not "so much", but EVERYTHING! For this, we give You thanks. In Jesus's name, Amen.

WEDNESDAY, MARCH 02

Let us pray; God of our fathers, Abraham, Isaac, and Jacob, You are from Everlasting to Everlasting and we worship You, our Lord. Guide us today. Help us study to be quiet, so that we may hear and learn. Search our hearts, renew our spirits, sanctify our minds. Show us how to humble ourselves before You, O fierce and mighty God, and each other. Let him who is the greatest among us be servant of all. We follow peace with all men, yet not compromising our lifestyle of true holiness according to Your Word. Bless us on this day with anticipatory expectations. Forgive us of our sins, in Jesus' mighty name, Amen.

THURSDAY, MARCH 03

Let us pray; Father of Mercies and God of all Comfort, we thank You for all the beautiful gifts You have bestowed upon mankind. These gifts are a blessing to us. They encourage and lift us in so many ways, at so many times. No one could have designed these gifts to accomplish Your purpose the way You have. We bless You now, because You make us happy; You bring us joy, O Thou Faithful Creator! We rejoice in You this marvelous, magnificent morning! Have Your way and we will be satisfied. In Jesus' name, Amen.

FRIDAY, MARCH 04

Let us pray; God our Father and the Father of our Lord, Jesus Christ, we bless You; Jehovah-Nissi, God our Banner; if God be for us, who can be against us? Go before us this day. Help us to seek after those things we cannot see; incorruptible things, where layed up in heaven for us is a crown of righteousness. Let us touch someone in need; not touching as to fulfill the lusts of the flesh, but to do the Will of our Father, that God be glorified. Turn our attention to You, Father that we may draw nearer. This is our prayer, in Jesus' name, Amen.

SATURDAY, MARCH 05

Let us pray; Father, we come before You with our hearts overflowing with joy; elated to be in fellowship and more important, Sonship with Jesus. How great Thou art! We honor You, adore You, magnify Your name, we lift You higher, ever grateful for Your love towards us. We thank You for this race we run; we sweat, stumble, trip, fall, grovel, stop, restart, complain, collapse, some have fainted...HAVE MERCY, please. Help us to keep our eyes on the prize to obtain, to win; not to come in first, but to finish well. Refresh us, dear Lord, in Jesus' name, Amen.

SUNDAY, MARCH 06

Let us pray; This is the day that the Lord has made; we shall rejoice and be glad in it. Our Father, we thank You for Your many blessings. If it had not been for You on our side, where would we be? It is of Your mercies that we are not consumed, because Your compassions fail not. They are new every morning: GREAT is Thy faithfulness. We honor You. Remember the downtrodden, the broken hearted, the confused, the deceived and misled; reset their focus on You and renew their strength that they may endure; we pray for direction in these matters and for their lives. This day is blessed and we declare and decree no weapon formed against us shall prosper. In Christ Jesus' mighty name, Amen.

MONDAY, MARCH 07

Let us pray; Our Father, the Unchanging, Eternal, Self-existent, Covenant Keeping God, we worship You, O Holy One. It is our desire to live a long and fruitful life according to Your Will. Help us to keep Your commandments. No longer under the law, but under grace, help us to walk circumspectly as true children of God; not bringing Christ to an open shame. Guard our tongues, guide our footsteps, govern our ways that we may please You and not man. Prosper us that we may have good success as we keep Your Word. We thank You for keeping back the hand of the devourer as You promised. This day is blessed, in Jesus' name, Amen.

TUESDAY, MARCH 08

Let us pray; Great Wonder Worker, God of all living and Lord of all creation, Excellent is Thy Name! We are thankful this morning for all You've done, are doing, and will do for us, Your people. We thank You for the great work You are doing in our lives. O God. Happy are we for the filling and the refilling of Your Spirit in us, hallelujah! You are the Potter, we are the clay, make us over, have Thine own way. We thirst after You in a dry and dusty land; fill us with the water from the well that never runs dry; You are that living water. Father, have mercy on us, cast our sins into the sea of forgetfulness and remember them no more; deliver us of our filthy thoughts and nasty ways that we may be able to do a good work for You. Clean us up. Provoke us, Almighty God, to take inventory of ourselves; therefore let him that thinks he stands, take heed lest he fall. We have been forewarned by

Your Word because of Thy Faithfulness. Help us, that our faith fails not. We seal this prayer in Jesus' name, Amen.

WEDNESDAY, MARCH 09

Let us pray; Gracious Father, thank You for the dawning of a brand new day. Thank You for giving Your angels charge to keep watch over us in the midnight hour. Blessed Father, when our minds were not regulated, when our hearts were hardened, when our bodies were out of sync, when our spirits were low, when finances were depleted, when we couldn't see our way, You stepped in and we thank You, our Covenant Keeper. Bless us on this day, keep us safe, have mercy on us, Your people, in Jesus' name, Amen.

THURSDAY, MARCH 10

Let us pray; You, who makes the sun to rise, the moon to stay in place, the stars to shine bright, the planets to keep their order; You, El Shaddai, the God who is more than enough; You, Jehovah Jireh, the all-providing One, You; You, who passionately increases hope; You, who holds the mysterion, the sacred secrets, and gives revelations as You will, You; in all the earth, under the earth, throughout the Universe, in and out of time, before and after time; we declare and pledge our allegiance to You, the One and Only, True and Living God; HOW GREAT THOU ART, EXCELLENT IS THY NAME! We love You. Keep us saved, in Jesus' name, Amen.

FRIDAY, MARCH 11

Let us pray; Our Lord, Our God, thank You for this day. Thank You for being mindful of us. Every provision has been made for us according to our faith. We thank You for divine favor. We rest in You and Your Grace. We find peace in Your Word. We thank You for Your Son, Jesus Christ, our Saviour. We thank You for His life, death, burial, resurrection, and ascension. We are looking for His return, to receive us unto Himself. Bless Your people all over the world. We seal this prayer in Jesus' name, Amen.

SATURDAY, MARCH 12

Let us pray; Blessed Father, we thank you this morning for all things wonderful. We ask that You keep our bodies healed. Help us to keep Your commandments and not to take Your Word lightly. Go before us on this day; lead us and direct us that we may do Your Will. Search our hearts, remove anything that is not like You. In Jesus' name, Amen.

SUNDAY, MARCH 13

Let us pray; Father, in the face of adversity, in the house of tests and trials, on the road of challenges and confrontations, we trust You. God, You have spoken and we accept what You allow, knowing that all things are working for our good. We seal this prayer this day, in Jesus' name, Amen. We love You, Lord.

MONDAY, MARCH 14

Let us pray; Father, You are a God who does what He wants to do and it pleases us. We look at You, Father and are amazed at how You work glorious wonders, right before the enemy's face on our behalf for Your glory; King David said in Your Word, "Thou preparest a table before me in the presence of mine enemies:..." (Psalm 23:5a KJV). Have mercy on us. We seek to please You in all of our ways. We pray for direction in all of our matters. In Jesus' name, Amen.

TUESDAY, MARCH 15

Let us pray; Heavenly Father, Creator, Ruler, and Maker of all things, we honor and praise You. We thank You for being God and Lord of our lives. Revive our tired bodies; renew our challenged hearts; restore our tried convictions; remind us of Your magnificent sacrifice of Your Son, Jesus, and His sacrifice of His life. Keep us ever humble at Your feet, never to think anything is of ourselves. We thank You for our faith which connects us to You. Blessed is this day, in Christ's name, Amen.

WEDNESDAY, MARCH 16

Let us pray; Father, we thank You for change; change of the seasons, change of minds, change of attitudes and ways, change for the better. Thank You for flexibility to change, it increases the joy of life; the passion for newness in life, it pushes us to higher heights in Christ and our calling. Thank You, Father for stability in You. Your Word says, "That we henceforth be no more children, tossed to and fro, and carried about with every wind of doctrine, by the sleight of men, and cunning craftiness, whereby they lie in wait to deceive;" (Ephesians 4:14). Thank You, again for stability. We praise You so much for stability. Stability, stability, stability is what we are grateful for in Christ, Amen.

THURSDAY, MARCH 17

Let us pray; Everlasting Father, Mankind Keeper, Almighty Redeemer, we thank You for Your undying love, Your "keep showing up on time" attribute, Your gentle touch in correcting us when we have gotten out of line, Your plumb line. Father, have mercy on us, deliver us from all appearances of evil. Keep us in Thy holy will. We love You and Your people. We thank You for Your Son, Jesus Christ being the Way, the Truth, and the Life. Help us to commune with You throughout our day, seeking Your direction in all of our matters. This day is blessed, in Jesus's name, Amen.

FRIDAY, MARCH 18

Let us pray; All Knowing, All Powerful, Ever Present God, the Shepherd and Bishop of our souls, we give You praise, glory, and honor for another opportunity to say thanks. We thank You for Your mercy, Grace, and kindness. In the midst of our troubles You are the only one good factor we can always depend on. For this we humbly acknowledge You. Have mercy on us as we strive to please You. Now unto the only wise God be glory and majesty, dominion and power, both now and forever, in Christ's name, Amen.

SATURDAY, MARCH 19

Let us pray, Dear Loving and Kind Father in Jesus' name, all glory be Thine. We remember the sufferings of Jesus; we go forth to Him outside the camp, bearing His reproach, we too, learn obedience by the fellowship of His sufferings. We rejoice, knowing we are partakers of His sufferings; that when His glory shall be revealed, we may be glad with exceeding joy for You granting strength to endure. For our light affliction, which is but for a moment, worketh for us a far more exceeding and eternal weight of glory. Father, we are not ashamed of the gospel of Jesus, for it is the power of God unto salvation to every one that believeth. Help us to continually spread Your Good News. For this and so much more, we thank You. Amen.

SUNDAY, MARCH 20

Let us pray; Father of All Light, Dispeller of all darkness, we thank You for rescuing us from out of darkness by the Great Sacrifice of Your Son, Jesus Christ because You are light. Now, we are lights; guiding the way for those still in darkness. Help all who are engulfed in a culture, worshipping they know not what. Have mercy, Father. Give all a mind, a yearning, a zealous desire to instead become engulfed in Your Holy Word. Help us to stop reverting into old habits, ways that are not beneficial to the Kingdom and our lives; because we have become tired, lazy, weary in this fight. Help us not to look on the faults, failures, and fears of others, but rather to search ourselves, crying out loud for Your help with our own insecurities and lows. Help us to guard our emotions and hearts. Help us to guard the gate to our lives, not allowing impermissible ones repeatedly dragging trash, clutter, unmentionables, and harmful debris into our history, causing delays, denials, doors shutting, spirits of depression, on and on and on...We need You to help us to hear the preacher, the prophet, the prolific messenger and message...Now is the time...the day you hear my voice...Come. We love You for being mindful of us, especially in our "in need of healing" processes. We believe and know You hear and receive this prayer, in Jesus' name, Amen.

MONDAY, MARCH 21

Let us pray; Dear Father, blessed are we; Your Grace is immeasurable. We thank You for Your Love; it knows no bounds; You spared not Your own Son so that we might have eternal life. Give us wisdom on this day. Help us to use our patience to wait on Your direction. We praise You now, for Christ's sake, Amen.

TUESDAY, MARCH 22

Let us pray; Father of All Generations who believe, Our God who hath no similitude, for there is none like You, we thank You for who You are and all that You are to us. We are Your people, You are our God; we walk by faith and not by sight, we are not of them that draw back; help us to be sober and watchful to the saving of our souls. Keep us safe in Jesus's name, Amen.

WEDNESDAY, MARCH 23

Let us pray; Father, if we say nothing else to You this day we say, "Thank You." Amen.

THURSDAY, MARCH 24

Let us pray; Merciful Father, as we reflect on the road to Calvary, as we abase ourselves with Christ, as we look to You who strengthened Christ to complete His task for our sake, we quietly join in commune with the Godhead, giving ourselves to Your Will. Thank You, for we are confident of this very thing, that You which hath begun a good work in us will perform it until the day of Jesus Christ... (Philippians 1:6). In Jesus's name, Amen.

Friday, March 25

Let us pray; O Our God, we thank You for this season. We embrace and cleave to the love and sacrifice You've manifested through the giving of Your Son, Jesus Christ. It is recalled and needful daily in our walk with You. We draw strength from the remembrance of the agony and the ecstasy, the pain and joy from the process of the task at hand. What joy in knowing we have completed that which has been assigned to us by God. What a mighty God we serve and such a wonderful Christ we worship. We thank You for opening the Way for us. This day is blessed and fruitful for Christ's sake, Amen.

Chapter Three

Lent Prayers 2017

Prep-prayer:

Tuesday, February 28

Good Morning and Blessings,

The season of Lent is the journey of Jesus towards the cross. It is the inescapable struggle of the wills of life and death. Yet, this is the way that leads to life. Lent begins tomorrow, Ash Wednesday. It continues for 40 days, not including Sundays. It is good to sacrifice, give up something you overindulge in, ie sweets, sodas, gossiping, fault finding, etc. and pick up something in an area of slack, ie bible reading, meditation, intercessory prayer, exercise, etc.

Lent is a "Wilderness" season. A season where you discover or re-discover your purpose in life, a season for denying the flesh and feeding the spirit man, a season when testing and temptations will try you on every hand, and a season of learning how to stop talking and to start hearing what God is saying to you (direction) in order to overcome the enemy. If your mind and heart is already set toward the Father, then your wilderness struggle has already begun. Jesus is our perfect example of how to go through the wilderness triumphantly. The wilderness prepares you for your cross. Learn the lessons of your wilderness.

A God inspired prayer will be sent out daily to encourage you. Remember, there is no spiritual growth without a spiritual wilderness!

Wednesday, March 01

Let us pray: Most Heavenly Father, we are humbled in Your presence and strengthened in Your light. As we go through this day, help us to remember who we are and Whose we are. Direct us, overshadow us, cleanse our hearts, and renew our minds for Your glory and our help, in Your Son Jesus' name, Amen.

THURSDAY, MARCH 02

Let us pray: Almighty Father, Just Jehovah;
Prepare us for the bearing of fruit even in the wilderness. For we, the just live by faith, not by sight. Forgive us for giving You the silent treatment when things don't go our way. Remind us of Your kindness towards us whilst in our contrary ways. Draw us nearer to Thee, in Jesus' name, Amen.

FRIDAY, MARCH 03

Let us pray: Righteous and Holy Father, blessed and peaceful are these words of worship that rise up to You on the breaking of this new day. Thank You, thank You, thank You. Guide our steps, polarize our thoughts, temper our tone and words that we may walk among men as the ordained Priests You have chosen us to be; for we are the light of this world. Help us to guide them that are lost. In Jesus' name, Amen.

SATURDAY, MARCH 04

Let us pray: Our Father, Elohim, Creator, Magnificent One; We bow before You in adoration and bask in the light of Your shining Glory! Before going any further, we ask for Your mercy, pardon us for every terrible thought, word, and deed, intentional or not, please, forgive us. Now, Lord, we seek direction from You for today that You are glorified in all we do and that the fruit of our labor is more than enough (that there may be meat in Your house), nutritious (food for our souls), is enjoyable, and may remain (does not dwindle or leave). All for Your glory, In Jesus' name, Amen.

SUNDAY, MARCH 05

Let us pray: Dear Lord, as we give You thanks at the close of this glorious day, we are grateful that You are mindful of us. Keep watch over us as we rest and sleep in the darkness of night. Renew and refresh our tired bodies for the tedious task on the morrow, trusting You'll spare our lives and delay Your coming for our sakes, in Jesus' name, Amen.

MONDAY, MARCH 06

Let us pray: GREAT and MIGHTY GOD, we worship You, praise You, adore You, magnify You, extol You, esteem You highly, withhold nothing from You, cry out to You...for we decree and openly declare, You are our God. Our hearts are fixed, our minds are made up and our focus shall not be moved from the cross while in this wilderness. A charge to keep I have, a God to glorify.

Father, we keep our minds stayed on Thee evermore, let nothing deter us from Your Will this day. We command that the flesh MUST die (our will) that Your Will be done. Do not allow us to come out of this wilderness with our flesh still in control, leading and guiding us. For if this happens, hell will be our eternal home. We seal this prayer and call it done in Jesus' name, Amen.

TUESDAY, MARCH 07

Let us pray: Our God, Our Life Source, Our Prime Mover; Thank You this glorious morning. Blessed be You God, the Father of our Lord Jesus Christ, the Father of mercies, and the God of all comfort; full of compassion. You, Father, who showeth mercy not to those without the gate only, but even to the ones inside the gate who innocently are caught in an error every now and then, but do not practice sin, Thank You, Father. Kind Master, make our bodies whole once again, that we may be fully functional and able to run and complete our assignments for You. We place our broken, bruised, battered, wounded, fractured, and gnarled bodies (both inside and out...both mind and body) beneath the everflowing blood of Jesus Christ which healeth us, and by His stripes we are healed! We open our mouths and speak boldly into the atmosphere deliverance and good health. Thank You Father for our deliverance, Thank You Father for our total healing, Thank You Father for setting us free, and To God be the Glory, it is so in Jesus' name, Amen.

WEDNESDAY, MARCH 08

Let us pray: Father, we honor and highly reverence You on the cusp of this brand new blessed day, and we thank You for allowing us to see it. While we have Your attention Father, help us to think on this matter of making good choices and wise decisions. Father, remind us daily to ask Your direction for all things, and not to take it lightly. Help us to learn how to wait patiently and productively until we hear from You, resting peacefully in knowing that if we don't hear anything, we don't do anything. Father, dispatch ministering angels to help us receive Your reply whilst we continually pray and trust You, and not to allow the enemy to provoke or intimidate us out of position, for You have not called us unto vanity. Do this for us Father coupled with sweet Grace, in Jesus' name, Amen.

THURSDAY, MARCH 09

Let us pray: Heavenly Father, Giver of all Life; We give You thanks and honor, glory and worship for all You have done, for You are truly WORTHY! Our request this morning is that You keep our focus on You today. That we will not be distracted from our assignments given to us by You. Strengthen us as we face our many trials, build us up where we are torn down. You said in Your Word, My grace is sufficient for thee: for My strength is made perfect in weakness. Right here, right now, Father, we are leaning on You who giveth us the VICTORY, in Your Son Jesus' name, hear and receive our prayer, Amen.

Friday, March 10

Let us pray: Kind Father, Loving Caregiver, Soother of our Souls: Rising this morning with breath in our bodies, movement in our limbs, the gifts of sight, hearing, smell, touch, taste, the blessing of a melodious voice, we praise Your mighty name for these and more, all to worship You! Thank You for these gifts. We thank You, Father for true leadership, those who we follow as they follow Christ. Continue to lead and direct Your leaders for Your glory and our sakes. Help us, Your people to be a help to Your leaders and not a hinder. Keep our minds stayed on You, help us to utilize what we've been taught. This day is blessed because we are still here. In Jesus' name, Amen.

Saturday, March 11

Let us pray: Omnipotent Wonder, Omniscient Majesty, Omnipresent Spirit, Our Father, Thank You for loving us, Thank You for continually loving us through it all, thank You. Everyday is a day of thanksgiving. We slack not on our worship and praise to You because You never slack on Your promises and Your Word to us. Sure enough, You keepeth the Covenant, we stumble...You keepeth it, we make excuses... You keepeth it, we get angry with You...You keepeth it. Lord God, help us to come to You and confess our sins and faults, that You may strengthen us for our journey. Now Lord, remember the backsliders and the unbelievers. Give them a changed mind towards You. Let them return and surrender swiftly before nightfall. Oh Father, receive our prayer in Jesus' name, Amen.

Sunday, March 12

Let us pray: O Lord, Our God, we thank You for the blessings of this day. Surely You are faithful and just to all who believe. We are excited about Your move and Your plans for us, Your people. Help us to stay focused while You continue to work in our lives for Your glory and our good. In Jesus' name we pray, Amen.

MONDAY, MARCH 13

Let us pray: Kind Father, Holy One, It is good to hear Your gentle, still voice in the quiet of the morning. Thank You Father for the dawning of a brand-new day. Have mercy on us, guide our footsteps, keep our thoughts and emotions so that we may keep Your ways and statutes. Lord, because we love You, help us to keep Your commandments, for this is right. Help us to seek a way to help somebody today in word and deed, in Thy Son Jesus' name, accept this prayer, Amen.

TUESDAY, MARCH 14

Let us pray: Most Holy God of this Vast Universe and ALL that our feeble, frail eyes cannot begin to imagine exists, we worship You on this frigid day. Father, whatever state we find ourselves in, You have given us choices; to change our locations to better, and You have given us the power and the authority to change the atmosphere! For Your Word says in Philippians 4:11...Not that I speak in respect of want: for I have learned, in whatsoever state I am, therewith to be content. Therefore, we seek Your direction BEFORE we make our choices... the bitterness of the cold, or the blazing heat of the day...Thank God for the challenges! For You helpeth me, Leadeth, and guideth me in Jesus' name, keep us safe this day, Amen. To God be the Glory!

WEDNESDAY, MARCH 15

Let us pray: Our Lord, Strong and Mighty, we honor You and thank You for the great love You have and show for us day by day. You continually strengthen us, You shield us from the fiery darts of the enemy, You lead us out of harms way, You hide us from our foes and their traps, and You protect us even from ourselves. Daily, we worship and praise Your name. Daily, we seek Your face and direction. Daily, we are grateful for the comfort of Your Holy Spirit. Your mercy endureth forever and we esteem You highly. Keep us Lord, as we go higher in You and draw nearer to the cross. In Jesus' name, Amen.

THURSDAY, MARCH 16

Let us pray: Gracious and Kind Sovereign One; we are grateful for the gifts and talents You have given and birthed in us for Your glory and not for our vanity. Help us to remember to help one another, to protect one another, to intercede spiritually for one another, to be slow to judge, but quick in mercy. God help us to see You in the bretheren, knowing Christ said, ..."Inasmuch as ye have done it unto one of the least of these my brethren, ye have done it unto me," (Matt. 25:40b). We love You and appreciate Your love for us. Continue to strengthen us in the faith, in Jesus' name, Amen.

FRIDAY, MARCH 17

Let us pray: Lord, Loving Father; It's a brand-new day, and we're grateful! What a marvelous morning, a wonderful week, an opportune time to lift our eyes upwards and with every fiber of our being, just worship! Nothing else on our minds, only You and Your love for us and worship. Not asking for anything, not complaining, just worship and this day is blessed. Thank You, Lord for being God, in Jesus' name, Amen.

SATURDAY, MARCH 18

Let us pray: Faithful Father, Have mercy on us, Your children. During this season in the wilderness, help us to master and apply the necessary disciplines needed to focus on our assignment(s) to meet Your purpose. This begins by humbling ourselves before You. Help us to let go of the old familiar people and things that are not slated to walk with us at this appointed time, or whose time has ended. Father, help us to recognize distractions in all forms and teach us how to turn and walk away. We thank You for Your longsuffering with us. We thank You, we declare and decree we have the victory! In Jesus' name, Amen.

SUNDAY, MARCH 19

Let us pray: GREAT God and Father who disperses mercy and grace liberally. Thank You again, for being mindful of us. Keep our minds stayed on You throughout this day. Be Thou glorified in all we do. Have Your way divinely as You keep us, mind, body, and soul. In Jesus's exalted name, Amen.

MONDAY, MARCH 20

Let us pray: O Thou Great Jehovah, Creator and Divider of all gulfs earthly, and divine, Blessed is Your name, sanctified is Your Word, Holy are Your Ways, Just and Righteous are Your judgements. We cry loudly for Your help, asking You to send ministering angels to help us through these trying times. Help us to patiently wait on Your directions. Renew the expectations of Your promises. Let us not forget that Your name is, "FAITHFUL". Help us to encourage one another in the faith, in Jesus' name, Amen.

TUESDAY, MARCH 21

Let us pray: Dear Lord; We thank You for this day. You've been ever faithful to us, Your people and we're grateful. Kind Father, today we are encouraging ourselves in our most holy faith to press toward the mark for the prize of the high calling of God in Christ Jesus. Our steps are heavy, eyes watery, thoughts cloudy, hearts heavy, but the God we know and serve, the God we trust, the Lord which is, and which was, and which is to come, who hath always ordered our steps will faithfully continue to order them. Our faith will not fail us. Now unto Him that liveth, and was dead; and, behold, He is alive for evermore, His name is True and Amen. In Jesus's name.

WEDNESDAY, MARCH 22

Let us pray: Loving Father, Great Provider; Mighty and magnificent are Your ways. We are in awe of Your excellent work and ways, and my God, Your timing, Your timing is impeccable. We thank You for looking out for us at all times. Go before us on this day, make the pathway straight. We love You, Father, help us to keep Your commandments, in Jesus' name, Amen.

THURSDAY, MARCH 23

Let us pray: Awesome and Fearsome God, thank You for being God. Thank You for meeting us in Your secret dwelling place. Wondrous are Your works before all creation. We bow before You in adoration declaring that You are the one and only True and Living God. We put all things under our feet that are not of You that we may run well the race set before us. We thank You that there is no lack in any area of the lives of us who honor You with the firstfruits of our substance which You give. Help us to stay focused as we intentionally take up our cross daily and follow Christ, in Jesus' name, Amen.

FRIDAY, MARCH 24

Let us pray: Precious Lord, Our Sole Succor, we bless You this morning for moving in ways we cannot comprehend. Your Word says, "For my thoughts are not your thoughts, neither are your ways my ways", Isa. 55:8. Therefore Father, we pray for our government official's. Catch the reigns of their minds that they may seek Your guidance. Give them God-conscious advisors for Your people's sake. Help us to stop criticizing and to start praying positively...death and life is in the power of the tongue...I shall declare and decree a thing. Father, we who have Your Holy Spirit dwelling within us have the power and the authority to bring change according to Your direction. Keep us covered under the shed blood of Christ, in Jesus' name, Amen.

SATURDAY, MARCH 25

Let us pray: Heavenly Father, we thank you for Your plans that You have for us today. Have mercy on us. Bless our going out and our coming in. Let us not be selfish with this salvation, but to speak life to some dying soul today, in Jesus's name, Amen.

Sunday, March 26

Let us pray: Bless God from Whom all blessings flow, Majestic Creator, Sovereign Watcher; On this magnificent, marvelous, monumental morning we lift holy hands to You, and say, "THANK YOU, FATHER FOR ALL YOU HAVE DONE!". This morning You've renewed strength, encouragement, joy, You've increased our enlightenment, obedience and understanding, wisdom and knowledge, peace, quietness, clarity, and given us a greater determination in Christ. Lord, Our Lord, have Your way in our finite lives while here on earth, use us to draw dying men and women to Christ. In Jesus' name, this prayer is sealed...Amen!

Monday, March 27

Let us pray: Our Father, we come this new day with penitent hearts and thankful spirits. We seek Your help, deliverance, and healing. Father, deliver us from still carrying old hurts and wounds, old mishaps and failures, torturing ourselves day after day. Father, heal our spirits of this mindset of self-destruction and self-sabotage. Father, we ask for Your help in letting go of the past that is not a help, but a hinder; letting go of people and things that make us get stuck; help us to not judge others, but to pray for their enlightenment. These are some requests for our betterment to be fit for the work of Your Kingdom. Now unto the only wise God, be glory and majesty, dominion and power, both now and evermore, in Jesus' name, Amen.

Tuesday, March 28

Let us pray: Heavenly Father, Giver of all Life; It is with great joy that we greet You this bright and wondrous morning. Our hearts and spirits are overflowing with gratitude for the love You have bestowed upon us. Help us to continue to strive and press towards the mark of a high calling in Christ Jesus. We are encouraged and excited to finish well this race, only with Your help. Help us to hold fast the integrity of the Lord's Kingdom as His Ambassadors in truth, mercy, and above all, love. In Jesus's name, Amen.

WEDNESDAY, MARCH 29

Let us pray: Our Father, thank You for life and the desire to live this morning. Thank You for Your Holy Spirit that leads and guides us. Order our steps this day. Keep us ever humble before You as You continue to strengthen and heal both our mortal bodies and inner man. Help us to stay focused, in Jesus's name, Amen.

THURSDAY, MARCH 30

Let us pray: Great and Mighty God, thank You for this day. Heal bodies, renew strength, set free the captives, give power to the faint, help those in need, remember the motherless and widows, encourage the fatherless, uplift the downtrodden and dismayed, restore Your joy; for the joy of the Lord is our strength. We are blessed because we trust You and the plans You have for us. Thank You for this love, in Jesus's name, Amen.

FRIDAY, MARCH 31

Let us pray: Bless God from whom all blessings flow, Majestic Creator, Sovereign Watcher; on this magnificent, marvelous, monumental morning we lift holy hands to You, and say, "Thank you Father, for all You have done!" This morning You've renewed strength, encouragement, and joy. You've increased our enlightenment, obedience and understanding, wisdom and knowledge, peace, quietness, clarity, and given us a greater determination in Christ. Lord, our Lord, have Your way in our finite lives while here on Earth, use us to draw dying men and women to Christ. In Jesus' name this prayer is sealed, Amen.

SATURDAY, APRIL 01

Let us pray: This is the day the Lord has made, we shall rejoice and be glad in it! Father, there is no one like You, and we thank You for caring for us. Thank You for hearing and answering our prayers. We thank You for good results. To God be the glory. As we come to the dusk of this day, and the blush of a new, keep us focused on You. Continue to use us to draw lost souls unto You, in Jesus' name we pray, Amen.

SUNDAY, APRIL 02

Let us pray: Most Gracious One, we thank You for the blessings of this day. We thank You for the sweet rest of this day. We thank You for the Holy Reverence of this day to You. Bless us now. Keep us according to Your Word as we keep Your Word according to Your statutes. Continue to have mercy on us and dispense Your Grace according to Your Great Wisdom. We are forever grateful to the One True God, Who gave His Son, Who gave His life that we may have a right to the Tree of Life, in Jesus' name, Amen.

MONDAY, APRIL 03

Let us pray: Heavenly Father; Great is Thy Faithfulness. Thank You for being a God Who keeps His promises. Blessed are we, the children of the Covenant, who You promised never to leave or forsake. Help us to stay focused and to fulfill our purpose, in Jesus' name, Amen.

TUESDAY, APRIL 04

Let us pray: Precious Lord; we are thankful this day for the riches of life and living. We are so grateful for Your unmerited favor in our lives. Father, strengthen us with Your joy as we fight this spiritual warfare with the spiritual weapons You have given us. Build us up in our most holy faith. Keep us as we do Your divine Will, in Jesus' name we pray, Amen.

Thursday, April 06

Let us pray: Heavenly Father, Giver of all Life; We give You thanks and honor, glory and worship for all You have done, for You are truly WORTHY! Our request this morning is that You keep our focus on You today. That we will not be distracted from our assignments given to us by You. Strengthen us as we face our many trials, build us up where we are torn down. You said in Your Word, My grace is sufficient for thee: for My strength is made perfect in weakness. Right here, right now, Father, we are leaning on You who giveth us the VICTORY, in Your Son Jesus' name, hear and receive our prayer, Amen.

Friday, April 07

Let us pray: O Benevolent, Gracious Father; we bless You for another day. This week has been VICTORIOUS!, all because of Thy faithfulness, grace, and mercy, so we thank You. The shield of faith has protected us; Your divine Wisdom has guided us; Your Holy Spirit has kept us; and Your anointed chosen spiritual shepherds have instructed us. Father, continue to inspire and be with us daily. Have thine way, in Jesus' name, Amen.

Saturday, April 08

Let us pray: Most Watchful Covenant Keeper, thank You for the beginning, interlude, and close of this glorious day. Thank You for the healing of our bodies, souls, and minds. Continue to help us as we stand against the wiles of the enemy. We are empowered by Your rhema word, so we open our mouths, declaring and decreeing Your Will which is Your Word. As You seal this night in history, we also seal this prayer and declare our requests done (make your requests known unto the Lord), in Jesus' name, Amen.

SUNDAY, APRIL 09

Let us pray: Father, we thank You for this day and all that it has blessed us with. We thank You for the movement of forward, because forward looks good on Your people. We thank You for the past, and now since our season has changed, so have our garments. We thank You for "...the garment of praise for the spirit of heaviness, that they might be called trees of righteousness, the planting of the Lord, that He might be glorified" (Isaiah 61:3b). We thank You for strongholds being broken today in Jesus' name. Save souls, Amen.

MONDAY, APRIL 10

Let us pray: Everlasting Coherer and Great Confirmer; we bless You for the body of Oneness. Though we are many, diverse, unusual, not the same, yet we embrace the multiplicity of gifts You have bestowed upon each of us, to bless each of us, to help one another, that You may be glorified in all of Your infinite Wisdom, because we are one. You confirm and cohere us in unity for our benefit and Your glory. For this we say, thank You. Help us as we meet and overcome the challenges of this week. Give us quiet to listen to others who come to us burdened, not so much seeking an answer, but a listening ear and compassionate heart. Thank You, Father for all You've done, in Jesus' name, Amen.

TUESDAY, APRIL 11

Let us pray: Our Father, we thank You for the purpose You came in the likeness of sinful flesh, to die in our stead that we may have a right to the Tree of Life. Your sacrifice and suffering will always be remembered. Thank You for being our final Pascal Lamb, Our Passover. To God be the glory. Keep us humble, keep us focused in our journey to do Your divine Will, in Jesus' name, Amen.

WEDNESDAY, APRIL 12

Let us pray: Our Father; we thank You for the sacrificial love You have for us, Your people. Draw us nearer to Thee as we stay focused on obeying Your Word. Thank You for the multitude of blessings; good fruit of our bodies, good produce of our land, whatever we put our hands to is blessed, good health, enemies defeated, we are the lender and not the borrower, the head and not the tail, we are above and not beneath, these and much more You bestow upon us from obeying Your Word. Continue to help us in the Joy of the Lord, in Jesus's name, Amen.

THURSDAY, APRIL 13

Let us pray: Heavenly Father, in Jesus' name, Grateful are we for this day and the blessings and lessons it brings. We thank You for Christ, Our Lord and Savior, who hung, bled, and died on Calvary's cross for our sins. Thank You for raising Jesus from the dead just as He said. What a mighty God we serve. Now unto Him that is able to keep us from falling, and to present us faultless before the presence of His glory with exceeding joy, to the only wise God our Saviour, be glory and majesty, dominion and power, both now and ever. Amen.

FRIDAY, APRIL 14

Let us pray: Creator, Sustainer, Provider, Watcher, Say-Sower, Harvest-Reaper, Healer, Sanctifier, Husbandman, Keeper, Incontrovertible God...Great is Thy Faithfulness! What shall we render unto You for all of Your benefits toward us, we will take the cup of salvation and call upon the name of the Lord...Jesus! Father, while on our jobs and during the course of this day, we will focus on what You've done for us; sacrificed Your Son, which left the greatest earth-shaking, sun-removing, grave-opening, most profound indelible line of demarcation in the annals of time. A perfected anomaly - the saving of mankind! This day by our faith every chain is broken, every stronghold is destroyed, all doubt is dismissed, and life reigns forevermore, in Jesus' name, we declare and decree, Amen.

SATURDAY, APRIL 15

Let us pray: Heavenly Father; we thank You for being God and for being mindful of us, Your people. Thank You for making it possible for us to have a right to the Tree of Life, Eternal Life with You. We thank You for giving us power and authority to do greater works after that the Holy Ghost is within us. Thank You for a mind to testify of Your Great deeds, the mighty works You have done for us in Jesus's name. Father, we anticipate greater, we joyfully welcome more, not only for ourselves, but for the brethren. Lord, remember our nation and those in command, have mercy. We pray for the peace of Jerusalem. We speak better days ahead, in Jesus' name, Amen.

Chapter Four

LENT PRAYERS 2018

WEDNESDAY, FEBRUARY 14

Our Father, Most Gracious and Kind One, Thank you for this blessed and wonderful day. As we remember the mortality of our bodies and the immortality of our souls, let us count up the cost of the lives we each live daily. This we ask in your Son Jesus' name, Amen.

THURSDAY, FEBRUARY 15

Heavenly Father, we bless Your name for all things new this morning. We ask for mercy and direction throughout this day, accompanied by Your ever-loving grace. Before we make choices and decisions, not just today, but everyday, help us to remember to stop and inquire of You in the way You would lead, instruct, and guide us. Father, remember the backsliders, return them home. Father, remember the brokenhearted, stop the bleeding, heal their wounds, and let it be for a testimony for Christ. These things we humbly request in Jesus' name, Amen.

FRIDAY, FEBRUARY 16

Righteous Father, Eternal One, we worship and glorify You this magnificent day. It is with awesome wonder that we rise to greet the sights and sounds of this blessed life, a life that could have been snuffed out at any time in the midst of our rest, but GOD...THANK YOU, LORD. We pray for those connected to the 17 lives taken in Parkland, Florida Wednesday, and we even pray for the young shooter; for we know that You are the Father of mercies, and the God of all comfort; Who comforts us in all our tribulation, that we may be able to comfort them which are in any trouble. Father, charge Your angels to go with us, keep us safe through the day and we give You the honor and the glory in Jesus' name, Amen.

SATURDAY, FEBRUARY 17

Father, in Jesus' name we appreciate all things new. Thank You for bringing us through another week whole; although challenged, tempted, and tried, it was the blood of Jesus Christ that covered us, and kept us right here another day. We Thank You Father as we look forward with anticipatory expectations, our hands lifted up, our heads held high, and our eyes fixed upon You to receive those good results to our answered prayers we've so long waited for...This is the prayer posture we are in today, full of joy and expectancy! Go before us on this day, make our pathway straight, and keep our minds focused on You, and we will forever give Your name the praise, Amen.

SUNDAY, FEBRUARY 18

Heavenly Father, Creator, and Keeper of our Souls, we bless You this morning for being God, then for loving us the way You do; nobody can love us like You! Thank You for the activities of our limbs and the functions of our bodies. Oh, we've had aches and pains, visits to the doctor, diagnoses, even surgeries, but You God, through the name of Jesus and by our faith, sustained, delivered, and healed our natural bodies. Now Father, through this same methodology, we are believing You for the same healing of our souls. Every bleeding wound, every broken heart, every messed up mind, every unforgiving spirit, every stuck spirit, every cancerous spirit, and every spirit that hinders us from moving forward in Your divine Will must submit. Father, we thank You for being our God, in Jesus' name we seal this prayer and call it done! Amen.

MONDAY, FEBRUARY 19

Glorious Father, Ancient of Days; we greet You this morning with a spirit of thankfulness, appreciation, and gladness. You have kept us yet another day and in our right mind. We thank You Father because there is no lack. We thank You for the former and the latter rains that You have given us abundantly. Our floors are full of wheat, and the vats overflow with wine and oil. Father, we thank You for restoring the years that the locust, cankerworm, caterpillar, and palmerworm have eaten. We thank You Father, for there is no lack! There is plenty and we are satisfied, and we praise Your name, for You have dealt wondrously with Your people and we are not ashamed. Father, bless us as we go forth on this day, in Jesus' name, Amen.

Tuesday, February 20

Almighty God, Omnipotent, Omniscient, Omnipresent One; We glorify You this marvelous morning for all that You have done. You have favored us...we could list the areas in which You've favored us, but just knowing that You've favored us at all is enough to go up in a blaze of glorious praise and worship! Thank You, Father for caring. As we embark on and progress through this day, guide our footsteps, polarize our thoughts, teach us Your ways, and please Lord, have mercy on us. These things we ask in Your Son Jesus' name, Amen.

Wednesday, February 21

Father, Holy and Righteous is Your name; We thank You this morning for Your Spirit of Peace, Your Spirit of Unity, and Your Spirit of Love. We thank You Father for the body of One; for in Christ we move as one, we speak as one, and we live as one according to Your Holy Word. Thank You Father for continually strengthening our mortal bodies so that we may be fit instruments for Your use any time, anywhere. This we ask in Jesus' name, Amen.

Thursday, February 22

Sovereign Deity, Everlasting to Everlasting, Our Father; We thank You this day for life, for giving us the victory, and always causing us to triumph in Christ. Father, we thank You for lifting; when the weight of this world and the cares of this life seem to be more than we can manage, You Father, through Your Holy Spirit remind us of

Your Word, "greater is He that is in you than he that is in the world", and "to whom much is given much is required". Father, we thank You for a fresh wind and the fresh oil. Prepare us for the journey, give us grace for the race, and mercy until the end. Bless us in Jesus' name, Amen.

Friday, February 23

Our Father, Magnificent Wonder; We extol You, we adore You, we magnify You, we appreciate You, we praise and worship You, and we love You. How marvelous are Your ways. We thank You for always being there for us, we may not always see You, we may not always feel You, but You're always there. Father, we pray this morning for our spiritual leaders all over this land. Keep them encouraged. Build them up in their most holy faith. Speak to them in the midnight hour. Keep their bodies healed. Continue to supply any need. Send laborers that will remain to the vineyards to assist with the harvest. Restore their joy. Rebuild the house and remind them that You've given them the city. Now, Father, as we follow Your leaders as they follow Christ, let us have the mind of Christ, and make of ourselves no reputation, but take the form of servants, humbling ourselves to the obedience of Your Will and Your Way. For we walk by faith, not by sight. This day is already blessed, in Jesus' name, Amen.

Saturday, February 24

Gracious and Benevolent Creator, Self-Sufficient One; Blessed art Thou Who gives comfort to troubled minds, strength to feeble and weak knees, sight to blinded eyes, hearing to dull and deaf ears, speech to a stammering tongue, and all needs are met according to our faith and Your Divine Will, for Your glory, and we thank You, we praise You, we give You honor, in Jesus' name. Father, help us to boldly witness and minister to someone who is in need today. Help us to lift Jesus higher. Father, restore our strength at the close of this week as we rest in Your Word and take comfort in the meditation of our heart, in Jesus' name, Amen.

SUNDAY, FEBRUARY 25

Holy Father, Excellent is Your Name; We are here this morning thanking and worshipping You for the Great God that You are. Bless us as we bless others. Father, we remember that great sacrifice You made for us by ransoming Your Son, Jesus that we might be reconciled back with You. We remember the great sacrifice Jesus made by giving His life for us as a ransom, a propitiation for our lives; thank You Jesus, O how Excellent! O how Faithful! Thank You Father, for raising this same Jesus, after being crucified for us, from the grave so that we may have eternal life. O how Excellent! O how Faithful! What more can we ask? We love You, Lord. We give You thanks in all things, Amen.

MONDAY, FEBRUARY 26

O Thou Great Jehovah; We greet You this blessed morning filled with new life just to give You glory. Father, we ask that You forgive us our trespasses as we forgive those who trespass against us. Thank You Lord, for the multitude of blessings You've bestowed upon us, even before we ask. Nothing we did was so profound to earn Your blessings, You simply choose to bless us, and Father, for this we are so grateful. Go before us on this day, direct our footsteps, help us to follow peace with all men, let us witness about Christ to some dying soul today as we lift Him higher. We pray this prayer in Your Son Jesus' name, Amen.

TUESDAY, FEBRUARY 27

Heavenly Father; We've gathered together in the spirit cumulatively, purposefully, and fervently, carefully and humbly before the threshold of Your throne. We have ascended here in the smoke of our daily prayers, requests, supplications, entreaties, petitions, confessions, communions, and intercessions by invoking the most Holy name, Jesus, the Christ. We submit unto You this morning special requests. Requests that we know only You can do. Requests that we need done quickly, suddenly. Thank You Father, we give You the glory, honor, and praise even before we see it because we believe, therefore; it is so. We seal this prayer in Jesus' name, Amen.

WEDNESDAY, FEBRUARY 28

Overly Generous One, Our God; We thank You for being so faithful to us, Your people. There is none like You. Father, we pray for our government; we pray for the legislative, executive, and judicial branches. We pray that You will intercede and intercept the plans of the enemy, speak to our president and his staff, and when You speak, make them hear You and obey You. Father, look on our Congress and House of Representatives, speak to their hearts, remind them that in writing and rewriting laws they are God's servants set in place to do God's Will for the good of all people; also, charge the judicial branch with Your understanding, do not allow them to interpret laws to suit man's will, but that it may fit the poorest of Your people. Father, bless the government of these United States of America for Your people sake, in Jesus' name, and glory, honor, praise, and Majesty belong to You, Amen.

THURSDAY, MARCH 01

Merciful Father, Hallelujah, Glory to Your Holy name; We bless You this morning, giving thanks to Jesus, our only living Saviour and Redeemer. Father, we receive by faith, the bountiful blessings that await us on this day, both naturally and spiritually. We thank You Lord, for favor this morning. Thank You Lord, for rebuking the devourer for our sake...thank You Lord, for the supernatural blessings of the giving of the tenth/tithe...so that we may be sure there is meat in Your house. Father, we pray for direction today. Help us to be sensitive to Your Holy Spirit. Charge Your angels to escort us here and there, as we journey through our day. We ask these things in Jesus' name, Amen.

Friday, March 02

Father, Our Father; As we near the close of another week, we lift our hands toward heaven and say, "Thank You". If it had not been for You Who was on our side... Lord, help us to stay focused on the tasks You have assigned us. Help us Lord, to run our own race that we may finish, and finish well. Father, open our eyes so that we might see how blessed we truly are. Keep our tongues from complaining, speaking negative, and fault finding. Let us see and acknowledge the good You've blessed us with. Keep us as the apple of Your eye, hide us in the cleft of the rock, and keep us sealed until the day of redemption, in Jesus' name we pray, Amen.

Saturday, March 03

Our Father, Great Awesome Wonder; We are overflowing with joy at hearing the mighty acts that You perform for Your believers. We thank You for teaching us how to wait on You and how to be productive in our waiting. Father, we thank You for knowing the value of praying that Your Will be done and not our self-will. Father, in the midst of all we go through, help us to remember to give You praise and honor first. Bless us on this day as we bless others, in Jesus' almighty name, Amen.

Sunday, March 04

Just, Holy, and Righteous God; We adore You for lifting us this morning with You on our minds. Because of how kind You are, keep us with a penitent heart and a mind like Christ. Father, we thank You for the blood-stained banner that still stands flurrying in life's winds. We thank for the plan and power of reconciliation, Hallelujah! Glory to God! Keep our minds stayed on You as we serve You throughout this day, in Jesus' name, Amen.

MONDAY, MARCH 05

Our Father, Keeper of our souls; It is one more day that You have blessed us to live and strengthened us to give You glory. Father, we thank You for a mind to serve You and our fellow laborers in Christ; not haphazardly, but with the fervent zeal of Christ, that we may win souls for the Kingdom. Righteous One, we ask that You search us this morning, anything that is not of You, take it out and replace it with more of You. Father, help us to do the work required for a closer walk with You. Settle us God, bring us to a state of maturity; purpose of intent: completion of this race. Father, direct us today as we give You glory, in Jesus' precious name, Amen.

TUESDAY, MARCH 06

Holy Father, Strong Tower, Mighty Fortress, Many Breasted One; You, Who are true, Who are everything and anything Your people need; We magnify Your most energized name; for the name of Jesus is fully charged with healing, deliverance, salvation; it is fully charged with freedom, overcoming power; it is fully charged with peace, love and war. Daily Father, we stand with the whole armor of God on, with our sword in our hand, prepped and ready for spiritual warfare. We decree and declare boldly, that we are reclaiming everything that the enemy has taken from us; our right minds, good health, a right standing with God, our children, whole families, riches and wealth, businesses, corporations, excellent jobs, neighborhoods, cities, states, countries, and everything unspoken that belongs to us! Father, cast us not away from Thy presence, but draw us nearer to Thee, in Jesus' name, we seal this prayer, Amen.

WEDNESDAY, MARCH 07

Kind Father; We are so thankful this morning for Your bountiful blessings. We made known our petition, we waited patiently and productively, and You answered our prayers. Father, we speak the sentiments of David in Psalm 116: "What shall I render unto the Lord for all of His benefits toward me? I will take the cup of salvation and call upon the name of the Lord. I will pay my vows unto the Lord now in the presence of all his people. Precious in the sight of the Lord is the death of His saints." Father, there is none like You! Hereto Father, with all going on around us, Daniel chases it with, "And all the inhabitants of the earth are reputed as nothing: and He doeth according to His Will in the army of heaven, and among the inhabitants of the earth: and none can stay His hand or say unto Him, What doest Thou?" Now Father, as Jesus did, we seal this prayer of thanksgiving with, "...let it be done on earth as it is in heaven," in Your Son Jesus name, we thank You, Amen.

THURSDAY, MARCH 08

Precious Lord, Eternal Justifier; Thank You for another beautiful and glorious day. Your blessings overtake us. We thank You Father, for Your joy because it is our strength. As we go through this day being directed by You, Father let us not be selfish and only think of someone else but let us do for someone else; let us meet their need. Lord, keep our bodies healed and fit for this journey, give us grace for this race, and grant us mercy to cross the finish line well. Now unto Him that is able to keep us from falling, and to present us faultless before the presence of His glory with exceeding joy, To the only wise God our Saviour, be glory and majesty, dominion and power, both now and ever. in Jesus' name, Amen.

FRIDAY, MARCH 09

Father, In the matchless name of Jesus; We come before You this morning in the spirit of humility telling You, thank You. Thank

You for Your mercy and Your divine grace; thank You for Your love towards us; thank You for Your long-suffering; thank You for Your deep compassions; and Father, in the midst of our tests and trials we thank You for understanding us even when we fall short. Now Father, strengthen my brother and my sister, lift them up and out of the valley of despair, reset their focus, renew their lease on life, restore their joy, and remind them that You've already given them the victory. Now thanks be unto God, which always causeth us to triumph in Christ... in Jesus' name, Amen.

SATURDAY, MARCH 10

Most High God, Possessor of All Heaven and Earth; It is once more that we come humbly before You, thanking You for all You've done and what You're going to do. Kind Father, we solicit Your mercy this morning for all deeds we've done and thoughts we've had that were not of You. Merciful One, as we go further into this year advancing towards destiny, bring us to a place of maturity. Father, reveal Yourself unto us, separate us, try our reins and our hearts; Father, take us higher. We thank You for this day, for it's already blessed, in Jesus' name, Amen.

SUNDAY, MARCH 11

Creator, Ruler, Sovereign Deity; We rise this morning with praise on our lips and thanksgiving in our hearts for You being God. Grateful that You gave us one more day to lift Jesus higher, for truly we owe Him praise. As we go forth on this day blessing and being blessed, give us edifying words to say, use our tongues for good and not evil. Teach us Thy ways O Lord, going forth to serve. Father, keep us in Thy holy will, in Jesus' name, Amen

Monday, March 12

Everlasting Father, O Thou Great Jehovah; We thank You for Your loving kindness and tender mercies toward us, for Your mercy endureth to all generations. We thank You Father for Your keeping power and Your glorious grace. We humble and abase ourselves before You, asking You to rekindle the mighty burning fire from heaven within us, stir up the gift of God which is in us, refresh in us Your Holy Spirit that we may finish our race well. Help us to stay focused on You as we go through this loaded week and we ask You to dispatch ministering angels to assist us with our multitude of assignments that You may be glorified and equip with Your Word us for this journey. Father, we love You, we give You the honor, glory, and the praise in Jesus' name, Amen.

Tuesday, March 13

Father, Master; All things are under Your domain, in and out of time. Everything that is, no matter where it is, or what, or who it is, is subject to Your Authority. Father, we thank You for hearing and answering our corporate prayers. Thank You Father, for the sudden manifestation of our finances, we thank You for our families uniting, we thank You for school grades going higher, Father, we thank You for the healing of our bodies and longevity, we thank You for enlarging our territory, and Father, we thank You for restoration. As we go forth on our assignments today O Lord, increase favor to accomplish that which is in Your Will. Father, we are watching the seasons and the times in Jesus' name, Amen.

Wednesday, March 14

Heavenly Father, Almighty Life Giver; This beautiful and blustery day we thank You for all the challenges that have increased our faith, strengthened us, that succor us without realizing it. Thank You Father for the challenges that draw us nearer to Thee, thank You for Your peace. Now God, You who command all elements, have mercy with the harsh conditions of weather all over the land, forgive us our short comings. Speak to the four winds to be calm, take the bitter bite out of the frigid temperatures, restore power where there is none, halt the flooding and drowning, and remind everyone everywhere that You are God and all things start and stop through You, in Jesus' name we ask according to Your Will. So, we honor You, we praise You, we give You glory, and Majesty, Amen.

THURSDAY, MARCH 15

Our Father; We are so grateful for Your goodness and Your mercy. You are with us at every turn. You God are our hiding place, our shelter from the storm; when the enemy tries to break into our camp, You God are there keeping him at bay for our sake. We run in to Your loving arms when we need an answer, a strong arm to lean on, because You promised never to leave us nor forsake us, and one great thing we know about You is that You are a Promise Keeper! Father, we thank You for our blessed and highly favored lives. We thank You for the comfortable church buildings You've blessed us to assemble and worship in. We thank You for our Shepherds who are leading us under Your direction. Go with us on this day, keep us hidden from all harm as we lift You higher, in Jesus' name we pray, Amen.

FRIDAY, MARCH 16

Our Father, Divine Covenant Keeper; We extol You high above any and everything. You, God who gives and fulfills dreams and visions through Your people, are great, and we thank You for being dreamers and visionaries after Your liking and purpose. We thank You Father for keeping us still as we watched You fight our battles. What a Mighty God we serve. We thank You for teaching us how to delight ourselves in You, while waiting on You, and You gave and are still giving us the desires of our hearts. What a Mighty God we serve, Father, we thank You. We thank You Lord for the press and the drive You've given us to do Your divine Will. Keep our bodies healed, restore the energy, strengthen us with Your joy, sanctify us through Your truth, make us one as You and Christ are one, and we are one in You. We bless You now in Jesus' name, Amen.

Saturday, March 17

Everlasting Father, our Most High God; we greet You this magnificent morning with enthusiasm and great expectations of all of Your promises. Thank You Lord for this day, another opportunity to witness to lost souls about Your love. Father, we speak healing to our mortal bodies, deliverance to our souls, and more than enough to our finances. Give us strength for the journey, in Jesus' name, Amen.

Sunday, March 18

Heavenly Father, we are thankful for this new and glorious day and for all of the bountiful blessings that are coming with it. Father, we owe You praise for Your goodness, Your mercy, and Your grace. We thank You Lord, for giving us the victory over the enemy, knowing that we are more than conquerors; for we know in whom we have believed, and we are persuaded that You are able to keep that which we have committed unto You against that great day. Blessed Holiness, continue to grant us traveling mercy, unmerited favor, and a closer walk with Thee. These things we ask in Jesus' name, Amen.

Monday, March 19

Divine Revelator, God of all Knowledge and Wisdom; Keeper of our thoughts and hidden secrets, Giver of good fruit in harvest time that remains; Lord, in these uncommon and uncertain times we worship Thee, drawing closer and closer still to Thee; giving thanks for the fruitful seasons of our lives. You're so gracious and kind to Your people with the abundance of overflow which causes no lack; for this we are thankful. Father, as we go through our day, we shall think on the sacrifice of our Lord and Saviour, Jesus Christ. We thank You for this time of reflections, hearing and believing the report of the brethren, having received our own personal experience with this same Jesus, we thank You, for when the fullness of time came, You made manifest Christ, our Redeemer, the Lion of Judah! Lord, we thank You for reconciliation, in Jesus' Righteous name, Amen.

TUESDAY, MARCH 20

Dearest Father; Let mercy guide Your hand today and grace touch here, there, and everywhere for our sake and Your glory. We thank You that we are not living in a state of not enough, but serving El Shaddai, God Almighty who is more than enough, who giveth us the victory to abundantly give to others in their time of need. Thank You Father for being our source. Be glorified this day through us Your people in deeds, not words, in Jesus' name, Amen.

WEDNESDAY, MARCH 21

Our Father; We bless You on this brand-new day filled with Your marvelous glory. We are grateful for being alive and well. Great is Thy faithfulness toward us. We acknowledge before You and all of heaven, a charge to keep we have, a God to glorify, a never dying soul to save, and fit it for the sky! Keep us ever armed and ready with Thy Word, willing and fit to do Thy Will. Remember those out of the ark of safety, use us to throw out the life line. Lord, help us, Your people, in Jesus' name, Amen.

THURSDAY, MARCH 22

Merciful Father, this day we are grateful for You being God. With You all things are possible and without You there is nothing we can do. Touch our mortal bodies with Your finger of love, cause divine healing to take place in Jesus' name we pray, Amen.

Friday, March 23

Most Holy, Just, and Worthy Father; Faithful and Excellent is Thy name; Thank You for just being God. Your blessings are abundant and perfectly timed, Your created beings still operate in accordance with Your Master blueprint, and we respond wholly when we submit to Your Divine Will. Thank You for answering prayers swiftly, fulfilling Your logos Word; "It shall come to pass, that before they call, I will answer and while they are yet speaking, I will hear." Go before us on this day, make the pathway straight, let us light the way for some lost soul, not so much in words, but more so in our daily life living. Be Thou glorified as we humbly submit this prayer in Your Son Jesus' name, Amen.

Saturday, March 24

Most Supreme One, He who causes us to rise and benefit, El Elyon, Possessor of Heaven and Earth; We worship You. Kind and generous throughout the night You have been to us. We remember and reflect on the sufferings of our Lord and Saviour, Jesus Christ, who took our place on Calvary's cross. We thank You for the plan of Salvation that we might be reconciled back to You through Christ. Grant us grace and we shall do Your Will this day in Jesus' righteous name, Amen.

Sunday, March 25

Father, Creator, Ruler, and Maker of all things; We bless and thank You for Jesus Christ, as we reflect on the agony of Him enduring the humiliation and shame brought upon Him falsely and unjustly, unworthily and unknowingly, but oh, so necessary. We thank You Father, for the power of His endurance. We thank You Father, for the power of His commitment. We thank You Father, for His power to subdue and conquer the flesh as He humbly surrendered step by step to the predestined, pre-allotted, and pre-tried Case of the Cross, not for Himself, but for us. Lord, help us this day to follow His example as we bear our cross for Your glory, in Jesus' name we pray, Amen.

MONDAY, MARCH 26

Our Father; We are filled with thanksgiving for all You have done. This day is blessed and full of miracles. We thank You for battles won that we didn't have to fight, we just stood still and saw the salvation of the Lord. Father, we thank You for Divine Favor in the courtroom, with those in high places. Let the outcome be favorable in Your people's direction, according to Your Will. We acknowledge You Father, our Supreme Judge, Who disperses justice as You see fit, and none can stay Your Hand. We seek Your direction today, as we humbly listen for Your voice with instructions. All these things we humbly ask in Your Son Jesus' name, Amen.

TUESDAY, MARCH 27

Father, Keeper and Deliverer; Great is Thy faithfulness unto us! We thank and praise You for a changed mind and a new heart! We thank You for the joy in bearing our cross for Your glory, knowing a crown, a royal diadem awaits us when we get over in glory land! Hallelujah! Philippians 1:29 says, For unto you it is given in the behalf of Christ, not only to believe on Him, but also to suffer for His sake. 1 Peter 4:13 and 19 adds, But rejoice, inasmuch as ye are partakers of Christ's sufferings; that, when His glory shall be revealed, ye may be glad also with exceeding joy; For I reckon that the sufferings of this present time are not worthy to be compared with the glory which shall be revealed in us. Father, we appreciate You for strengthening us while we're going through for Christ, and many times we didn't even know it. To God be the glory! This day, we thank You for strength in Jesus' name, Amen!

WEDNESDAY, MARCH 28

Father; We bless Your name on this day. We thank You Lord, for the healing of our bodies, souls, and minds. Your Word is forever faithful and true. Keep us focused as faithful witnesses for You; let us boldly make known Your deeds among the people, for we overcome by one another's testimony. Thank You Lord for life, good health, abundant riches and wealth, sharing spirits, compassionate hearts, teachable spirits, and the Spirit of Oneness. Bless our natural and spiritual leaders here, there, and everywhere. Remind us to pray Your Will and Word, not our will. We ask for direction on this day. These things we humbly request of You, in Your Son Jesus' name, Amen.

THURSDAY, MARCH 29

All Divine One, Self-Existing Ruler, The I Am; Great and Mighty are Thy works; great in counsel, great in purpose, great in deeds. We thank You, the One True and Living God, our Father, through Whom all existence is, was, and will be. This glorious, rich, and opportune filled day we purposefully seek to please and glorify You in all we say and do. Remember those who are without the gate, those who have lost their way, those who have lost communication with You for reason of doubt, lack of faith, misplaced blame, self-shame, and any and every cancerous reason that causes them to have unforgiving, bleeding, stuck, and unyielding spirits. Please Father, throw out Your lifeline, through Your masterful ways, use us to reach that soul before it is too late. Heal, set free, and deliver. Have mercy, grant grace and divine favor in Jesus' victorious name, Amen.

FRIDAY, MARCH 30

Heavenly Father, Just and Wise God; We bless Your holy name for Your keeping power. Keep us covered with the blood of Jesus Christ. As we ask for mercy, Father search our hearts, remove everything that's not like You. We thank You for the joy and peace in serving You. Thank You for revealing Yourself to us so that we might know

Who we serve. We thank You for the joy of the Resurrection, the help of Your Holy Spirit, and the overcoming, delivering power of Your Word through obedience. Now Lord, continue to strengthen us as we invoke Your name for direction while bearing our cross for Your glory. While bearing our cross, we still have strength to help somebody and lead them to You. As we humbly breathe the breath of life, receive this prayer in Jesus' life changing name, Amen.

UNTIL...

Printed in the United States
By Bookmasters